MONICA

ALSO BY NANCY ANN RICHARDSON

With Julie Krone
Riding for My Life

With Bela Karolyi
Feel No Fear

MONICA

FROM FEAR TO VICTORY

Monica Seles

with Nancy Ann Richardson

HarperCollins*Publishers*

HarperCollins books may be purchased for educational, business, or sales promotional use. For information please write: Special Markets Department, HarperCollins Publishers, Inc., 10 East 53rd Street, New York, NY 10022.

FIRST EDITION

ISBN 0-06-018645-3

96 97 98 99 00 RRD 10 9 8 7 6 5 4 3 2 1

This book is dedicated with love to
my mother, father, and Zoltan

ACKNOWLEDGMENTS

It is difficult to love with arms open wide enough to hold without crushing, mind clear enough to understand without judging, heart big enough to give without expecting to take. But that is what my mother, father, and brother have done throughout my life. Without their love and support this book, let alone my tennis career, would not have been possible. More importantly, I would not have had the sense of security and balance that has guided me even when my path wasn't clear. It does not seem enough merely to acknowledge my family's involvement and influence. Yet all I can say is, they are my light.

And then there's Betsy Nagelsen, a truly giving human being whose friendship is simply invaluable; Mark McCormack, whose kindness and guidance have helped me stay in the game; Dr. Steadman and Dr. Hawkins, whose expertise and compassion repaired my body, and Topper Hagerman and John Atkins, whose physical therapy and desire to care for my flagging spirits helped me toward recovery; Dr. Jerry May, who listened tirelessly, counseled wisely, and cared enormously; and my manager, Stephanie Tolleson, who continually backs me and makes all things possible.

To all these people, and to the tennis fans who have supported me throughout my career — even when times were tough — I can only say thank you. But I say those two words from my heart. Thank you.

Monica

My thanks to Monica for sharing her incredible story with me — a tale so full it's hard to believe her life has only just begun.

Much thanks to Betsy Nagelsen for her time, insight, and four tapes, and Mark McCormack for his editorial suggestions and ideas. And thanks to Mark Reiter, Stephanie Tolleson, Linda Dozoretz, Tony Godsick, Dr. Jerry May, Dr. Steadman and Dr. Hawkins, and Dr. Danelzik for their expertise and assistance.

And, as always, thanks to Jane, Art, Sue and my new brother, Peter.

Nancy

LIST OF ILLUSTRATIONS

A moment of glory: beating Martina Navratilova to take the US Open in September 1991 *(AP/Wide World Photos)*

Center of attention: proudly displaying to the Press the US Open Trophy, which I won for the second time in September 1992 *(AP/Wide World Photos)*

And, in January 1993, the Australian Open trophy I won for the third consecutive year *(AP/Wide World Photos)*

Giving a tennis lesson at the Special Olympics in 1995 *(AP/Wide World Photos)*

With Astro in Vail in 1993 during my recovery from the attack *(Seles archives)*

With my agent Mark McCormack and my mother on the way to the 1995 Atlantic City Exhibition, my first public game since the attack *(Seles archives)*

A warm gesture of support from Martina Navratilova after the Atlantic City Exhibition *(AP/Wide World Photos)*

Sharing the happiness at my return to tennis: reaching around a police guard to shake hands with a supporter at Atlantic City and signing autographs for tennis enthusiasts at the US Open, September 1995 *(AP/Wide World Photos)*

At the 1996 Special Olympics with Sonya Bell, the thirteen-year-old blind gymnast whose determination and fortitude inspired me *(Seles archives)*

Enjoying myself at a nightclub with Anke Huber and Mary Joe Fernandez after the 1996 Australian Open *(Seles archives)*

I used to wish that life was like a fairy tale. Once upon a times, happily ever afters, princesses, castles, dragons, and knights on stallions as white as snow. In fairy tales evil is always defeated and spells are broken with a solitary kiss. But the real world is not a fairy tale. And happily ever after isn't preordained. That's life . . .

I remember thinking that things couldn't be better; that the decision to enter the late-April Citizen Cup tournament in Hamburg in order to prepare for the French Open in June had been right. My whole family was there. It was the first time my brother, Zoltan, had come on a trip to Europe with me. We'd had so much fun at the January 1993 Australian Open that he'd agreed to be my hitting partner in Hamburg. Before the tournament began we spent time walking beside the beautiful lake by our hotel. It was sunny, beautiful . . . almost perfect.

There was only one worry: I thought I might not be in good enough shape to play. After a long virus that had kept me off the courts through March and early April, I was feeling weak. I went into my first few matches slightly nervous — hoping to play well and give myself confidence for the French Open. I did win my early rounds, but I wasn't satisfied with my performance. "More practice, Monica?" my father asked. I had a match late on Wednesday, but we went to the stadium to train that morning, anyway.

I had requested a strong security team from the tournament director of the Citizen Cup following an earlier problem in Germany involving a man who attempted to serve me court papers. Each morning at 6:45 am, a team of four men was supposed to meet me at the gates of the stadium and stay with me throughout my practice. Every day the team was at least ten minutes late. On Wednesday they didn't arrive until 7:40 am.

"So sorry," the security team said when they reached the court; "we overslept."

"Geez, these guys are getting paid, and they're not doing their job," I grumbled to my father.

I won my match that night. On the way back to the hotel my driver (a German student) told me that he thought we'd been followed from the stadium. "Put your seat belt on, Monica, I'm going to try to lose him." For the next half hour we sped along the Autobahn at breakneck pace. Tires squealed as we hurtled around corners and through hairpin turns. The small dark car that had been tailing us stayed on our tail. We couldn't see the driver — only that he was alone in the car. Eventually my driver gave up and took me to the door of my hotel. The dark car wasn't in sight as he escorted me to the lobby.

That's never happened before, I thought nervously. If someone just wanted an autograph, they could've asked. I never refuse. That night I had trouble falling asleep.

We went back to the courts on Thursday morning (April 29) for some more practice. This time only one of my four guards showed. Moreover there were several people in the stands watching my session. It was strange that spectators would get up that early just to watch me hit. How did they get into the club? I wondered. I tried to focus, but there was a man videotaping me. My brother went over to the guy and asked him not to record, telling him that I'd be happy to sign an autograph later. It took several requests, but finally the man stopped taping. I couldn't lose a growing sense of unease, and we ended the practice early.

"I'm just going to change in the locker room," I called over to my dad. Then I walked toward the tunnel that led to the lockers. There was a man in the stands to one side of the passageway. He was wearing an Arthur Ashe baseball cap — it was nice to see Arthur was remembered in Germany, too. The man in the cap leaned over to watch me pass. I looked up and smiled, and the man smiled back. I've seen that guy before, I recalled as I walked into the dimly lit tunnel. He was in my hotel lobby yesterday. What a coincidence. I hurried to change my clothes and meet up with my father and brother.

I didn't know that while I'd been hitting with Zoltan, my dad had also recognized the man in the baseball cap from the hotel. He walked over to him as he perched on the fence behind my court. "Nice weather in Hamburg," Dad said to the middle-aged guy. The man smiled but didn't respond. My father considered inviting him inside the fence so that he could watch my practice from an unobstructed view, but Zoltan warned that the invitation could compromise my security.

That night my father began to feel sick. We thought he might have the same virus I'd had the previous month. By noon the next day he was so ill that he couldn't come to my quarterfinals match against Magdalena Maleeva of Bulgaria. My mother decided to stay at the hotel to take care of Dad. Zoltan stayed too, but said he'd try to come halfway through the match to watch the end. "No big deal," I told Zoltan as I left for the stadium. "Just come if you feel like it."

The match didn't begin until 5:00 pm. The day had been clear and crisp, but with the sun weakening it was cold on the court. The first set was tough. Magdalena is a very good back-court player, and I fought to take her, 6–4. Then I fell apart. I was down 0–3 in the second set, and losing all control of the match.

What's going on with my game? I wondered. Concentrate and get back into this match before it gets so dark they postpone it until tomorrow morning, I told myself. If that happened, I'd have to finish the quarterfinal match in the morning, and if I won I'd play my semifinals match the same afternoon. I didn't want to be too tired to play well. I struggled until we were tied, 3 all. There was one more game before the changeover. I took the game and was up, 4–3. I went to my chair for the sixty-second break.

It was chilly. I moved my feet back and forth as I wiped cold sweat from my neck. Concentrate so that you can finish this in two sets, Monica, I told myself. I put my towel over my face and leaned forward to block out any distractions. My feet continued to shuffle. Just a few more seconds and it's time to get up, I thought. And then there was an incredible pain in my back.

It was sudden, sharp — a burning point on the left that radiated pain across my back and down my right side. There was a scream that was more animal than human. An anguished cry I hardly recognized as my own, even as it echoed in my ears. What is happening? I looked back over my left shoulder and saw a man in a baseball cap holding a bloody knife in both hands. He raised his arms above his head to strike again. In that split second I recognized his face from the hotel, remembered him from the empty stands. A security man grabbed him from behind in a headlock. His face got very red and I turned away.

I don't know when I stood up, or how I stumbled toward the net. I wasn't running away, because I was too deeply in shock to have any rational thoughts. A spectator was the first to reach me. He jumped down from the stands and held me by the shoulders. I began to feel dizzy and collapsed onto the red clay. The pain in my back was agonizing and I reached around to touch the spot. When I withdrew my hand it was slick with blood.

Trainer Madeleine Van Zoelen appeared. I asked her what had happened, but couldn't hear her reply over the drumming in my ears. Everything was happening too fast for my mind to catch up. Then I saw my brother race out onto the court. He came after all, I thought dully. I didn't ask any questions after I saw Zoltan. I knew he'd take care of me.

Looking back, I'm amazed they let Zoltan onto the court. None of the security guards or officials at the tournament knew he was my brother. Just as no one knew the spectator who had leapt over the railing to help me. If he'd been a friend of my attacker, he would have had more than enough time to finish the job. It just shows that security was so loose that anyone could have come on to the court.

But I didn't think any of these things at that moment. I focused on Zoltan's words: "It's going to be all right, Monica," he said as he rubbed my legs. "Keep moving, keep moving." And then, to the disorganized crowd around me, he cried, "Someone help her!"

My eyes caught Magdalena Maleeva — a solitary figure on the other side of the court.

"Monica, hang in there, hang in there," Zoltan urged me as Madeleine put pressure on my wound.

I was gasping. I couldn't get air. I couldn't breathe enough to tell anyone I was having trouble breathing.

"Come on, come on!" Zoltan called to the people around us.

I remember hoping that someone would give me oxygen. No one did. I was finally lifted onto a stretcher and wheeled off the court. Zoltan ran beside me toward the ambulance, which had been a long time coming.

"Mom and Dad . . ." I gasped to Zoltan as the paramedics laid me on my side for the ambulance ride.

"They'll be at the hospital," Zoltan promised as he rubbed my arms and legs to keep my circulation going.

There were so many thoughts racing inside my head: the word *stabbed*. I'd never said that word before; never even thought it. But I'd seen the knife. The knife had been inside my back. In and out . . . I'd been stabbed. Breathe, Monica. Breathe. The ambulance ride lasted forever. Madeleine rode with us to the hospital. She was very kind, and I was really grateful for her presence.

My parents were there when I was wheeled into the emergency room. Zoltan had called them. I can't imagine how helpless that made them feel. They were crying when I saw them — too frightened for their child to attempt to look strong.

I was taken into the examining room. After that, everything came in flashes of terror and pain.

2

I was out of my mind. After the German doctors had cleaned my wound, they decided they needed an MRI to determine the extent of the damage. I was wheeled into a small room and placed on a thin platform that was meant to roll into a large round cylinder.

"I can't go in that thing!" I cried as the nurses moved me toward the MRI machine.

"You have to so that we can see how bad the stab wound is," one of the nurses tried to explain in broken English.

"I don't care," I sobbed. "I can't lay down on my back like you want me to — it hurts too much."

They wheeled me in anyway. It felt as if I was in there for four weeks, not forty minutes. I was trapped and in a lot of pain. The nurse kept telling me not to move, but it was hard to stay in the same position because my back ached terribly. The doctors determined that the damage was to the soft tissues and muscles by my scapula. The wound itself was one and a half inches deep. The point of penetration was millimeters from my spine.

"You're lucky, Ms. Seles," one of the doctors explained. "If the blade had been a hair's breadth to the left, you might have been paralyzed."

By the time I was taken to a hospital room I was in a state of exhaustion. Still, I couldn't close my eyes.

What if he comes back? I thought in terror. What if he wants to hurt me again? At that point, I didn't know who "he" was, or that the man who attacked me was in custody. There was a guard at my door, but I asked my parents and my brother to stay by my bed. Having my family in the room made me feel safer. Finally the doctor prescribed some medicine to help me to relax and to take away the pain. I fell into a fitful sleep.

It didn't last long. Every few minutes someone knocked on my door. Zoltan would jump up and slip outside to see who it was. Then he'd return and I'd ask him really paranoid questions. I didn't trust anybody that night. And I didn't want to talk to anyone but my family. The press wanted a statement, but I had nothing to say. Some guy had just tried to kill me. I wasn't in the mood to talk about how and why. Unfortunately, you can't say no to the police.

The woman police officer walked to my bedside and began to ask questions. I was still in shock, and I couldn't follow her. I started to cry.

My brother interrupted the interrogation. "Leave Monica alone," he said to the cop. "I don't think it's the right time to talk to her — she's still in shock. Please come back tomorrow." He led the policewoman toward the door and grudgingly she left the room.

"Monica, the man who did this is in custody," Zoltan told me when he returned. "You're safe."

I didn't really register what he was telling me. I nodded, but I was still worried that the attacker would find my room in the hospital; that if I went to sleep, I'd wake up and see his face. I began crying again — it was something that happened all too frequently in the next two years.

"Why did he attack me?" I finally asked Zoltan.

"They're not sure, Monica," he replied. "Only time will tell."

None of it made any sense. I started to shake all over, and my mom crawled into my hospital bed and held me. The nurse wheeled in extra cots for Zoltan and my dad, who was still feeling very sick. That night we all slept in my room. As always, we dealt with the situation as a family.

On Saturday morning Stephanie Tolleson, my sports manager from International Management Group (IMG), arrived from the United States. Stephanie was going through a difficult pregnancy at the time and the flight had posed a risk for her, so I was really surprised to see her. It meant so much to me that she had come to Germany to help me to handle the situation: I'd known her since I was a junior player in Yugoslavia, and Stephanie was like family.

The hospital was filled with media. In the past I've made statements to calm certain situations. This time I didn't care whether my silence made things better or worse. I was just trying to cope. While I stared out the window of my room and thought about what had happened, IMG was busy working on a press release.

The media had been given misinformation by the hospital regarding my wound. Their description of the injury caused by the knife was not only incorrect; it trivialized my wound to the point where it became nothing more than a "slight cut." Unfortunately, it was much more than a flesh wound. I had been regarded by the media and my opponents as one of the most tenacious and tough players on the tour. But this was the hardest situation I'd yet faced.

Just yesterday I was focused on the French Open, I thought in amazement as I lay in my hospital bed. I was sure that I had a good chance of defending my Grand Slam title and maybe of becoming the first player in the world to win four consecutive French Open championships. Just yesterday I was the undeniable number one player in the world. Now everything had changed. I was no longer the strong person I had been twenty-four hours previously.

The next morning the world number two ranked player, Steffi Graf, came to see me. I was so glad to see her: she was my toughest opponent and I'd taken the number one spot away from her. When she walked over to my hospital bed, we both started to cry. I looked up at her, this woman who never showed emotion, and watched the tears fall. It was such a weird moment — two athletes staring into each other's eyes and crying.

Steffi said, "I'm so sorry that this happened in my country. Stay strong, you can get through this, Monica."

I looked up at her as she spoke — I still didn't know that I'd been attacked by a man who wanted to restore Steffi to number one. Not that it would have changed that moment.

"Well, I have to go because I have to play my semifinal match soon," Steffi said after we'd spoken for five minutes.

I stared up at her in confusion. They're going to continue the tournament? Why? I can't be there — nobody can play if I can't play, I thought as the tears flowed. I mean, a player just got stabbed at an international event. How could the tournament director act as if nothing had happened and continue with the Citizen Cup? I wished Steffi good luck.

As she left the room, she said, "I'll call you."

There was a lump in my throat I couldn't swallow. The tears kept flowing.

I was not the only one who was shocked to learn that the Citizen Cup would continue. My feelings were confirmed as I looked out my hospital window at the hundreds of sports-lovers who'd gathered to protest against the decision. The Citizen Cup was an international tournament, and I, a guest of the organizers, had been attacked during a match. It was unfathomable to those fans that the tournament would play on as if nothing had occurred.

Tournament officials called my mother at the hospital and asked her to address the sports fans who had gathered at the tennis center. They were protesting the continuation of the tournament after my attack. At that point she was exhausted, and so worried about me that she agreed to help and drove to the center. At a very difficult time, my mother stood in front of a crowd holding signs saying STOP THE TOURNAMENT. My mother said that for a moment everything went dark before her eyes, and it was only the kindness of some of the protesters, who hugged her and gave her flowers and teddy bears for me, that gave her the strength to address the crowd.

The fans were quieted, but the tournament officials' decision to continue the Citizen Cup met strong criticism from around the world. In addition, my own expectation that the players would unite and refuse to continue the tournament was shared by countless others. I was sad that the players chose to act as professional athletes, not human beings. Had another player been attacked, I would never have continued the tournament.

An hour after Steffi's visit, there was a loud pounding on my hospital door. My mother was in the bathroom, and my brother and dad had stepped out of the room. Maybe they'll go away, I thought as I huddled in my bed. There was another knock. I got out of bed and slowly moved toward the door to hide. Pain rippled down my side with each movement. I tripped over several plastic bags stacked against the wall. My sweats tumbled out along with a baseball cap. The name ARTHUR ASHE was written across the front of the cap. How did that get here? I thought in terror. It was a question I'd never be able to answer. I cowered behind the door, terrified that the man who had stabbed me had found my room. I wasn't thinking about the guard in the hallway — over-whelming terror flooded my senses.

The door swung open and the policewoman from the previous night strode in with another officer. When I saw who it was, I moved out from behind the door and shuffled back to my hospital bed.

When I was back in bed the policewoman placed several large plastic bags on the night stand. The male officer began to translate as she spoke. "We need to show you the evidence we've collected," he began. "You must tell us if these things belong to you."

The woman opened one of the bags and pulled out my bloody tennis shirt. It was in tatters, because the doctor had cut it off my back in the emergency room. The smell hit me first — dried blood, stale sweat; it filled my nostrils and clouded my head.

"I want my family," I gasped.

"Is this your shirt?" the officer asked.

"Yes," I said softly.

"And this?" the officer asked as the policewoman picked up another bag, opened it, and pulled an item out. "Is this the knife the attacker used?"

I stared at the nine-inch curved, serrated boning knife. There was dried blood on the blade. I heard the scream, animal-like and agonized in my ears. Over and over again, the scream. I looked down at my blood-encrusted shirt, tried to shake the stench from my senses.

"Ms. Seles, is this the knife?" the officer asked again.

I must have said yes, because he replaced the items in their bags and they both left the room. I started throwing up. My stomach convulsed again and again until there was no food left and I retched dry and bitter. And still nothing could get rid of the smell, or the knife, or the fact that I'd been stabbed. Nothing could change the reality that the tournament had gone on as if the attack had never happened. As if it didn't matter . . . I didn't matter.

Steffi Graf played in the semifinals of the Citizen Cup in Hamburg. "I'm not afraid," she told the press. "Tennis players have more or less been put on a stage. I think we need to be even closer to the people who watch us. You can't live with fear."

I was amazed by Steffi's calm reserve and bravery. Her words were incomprehensible to me, and her decision to continue the Citizen Cup tournament in spite of the stabbing shocked a lot of people. Personally, I was in awe of her mental strength.

Steffi Graf lost to Jana Novotna in the semifinals of the Citizen Cup in a tough, three-set match.

3

STATE CRIMINAL INVESTIGATION DEPARTMENT (LKA) 211
Hamburg, April 30, 1993

Re: Suspicion of attempted murder of Monica SELES; here:

TESTIMONY OF THE PERSON RESPONSIBLE [GÜNTHER PARCHE]

"I have just read through the declaration concerning testimony and understand that I do not have to make a statement to the police regarding the accusation. Moreover, at the very beginning of our conversation the officer taking the testimony advised me that I do not have to make a statement. However, I want to give my story and do not wish to bring in a lawyer at this point. I do not think that I need one.

"Before I begin my testimony, I want to say in advance that I am a great fan of Steffi Graf. I follow her entire career with great interest. I have, for example, been sending her money every birthday since the borders were opened. For the last two years I have sent her DM100, this year DM300. Moreover, I sent DM50 to her mother so that she could buy her a beautiful bunch of flowers on June 14 with the money. I always sent the money anonymously. All I ever wrote on it was 'a fan from Thuringia.'

"Then in 1990 Steffi Graf lost to Monica Seles in the German Open in Berlin. My world collapsed around me at that time. I could not bear the thought of someone beating Steffi Graf. Although she had not lost her number one seeding at that time, it affected me so much that I even considered suicide. What upset me the most was that she had lost in Berlin. If it had happened

anywhere else it would not have been quite so bad. She had already lost the occasional tournament elsewhere. But in this case it was in Germany, and even worse, in front of our Bundespräsident. That was all too much for me.

"In 1990 I also wanted to go to Paris for the French Open. But my journey was halted in Stuttgart because I did not have a valid passport to travel in France. Whether I was already harboring the thought of hurting Monica Seles in 1990, I cannot say for sure. In any event, I was really upset when Monica Seles won the French Open.

"In 1991, or 1992 at the latest, it was old news. I had then definitely decided to injure Monica Seles in such a way that she would no longer be able to play tennis, or at least not for a while. I want to point out here that at no time did I intend to kill her. I did not even want to cause her a serious injury. My only concern was to injure her so that she would not be able to play for a certain time. By doing so I would have helped Steffi become number one again.

"At this point I also want to say that the USA and Israel are my favorite countries. I am a great fan. But Steffi Graf is still at the very top. To me, she is worth far more than all the others. I would walk through fire for the USA, but for Steffi I would do much much more. For me, Steffi is the top woman. She is not only an absolutely top sportswoman, but she is also a unique woman. Her eyes sparkle like diamonds. She is an absolute dream woman. I really want to emphasize that; it comes straight from the heart.

"On Tuesday morning I left home and set off for Hamburg; I traveled by train. I went to a good hotel there, and I spent three nights there. I do not want to say which hotel it was, however. The people were so nice to me, and I do not want to get them into trouble. At Rothenbaum I bought a day-ticket every day. It was always a ticket for center court. I went to Hamburg to injure Monica Seles so that she would not be able to play tennis for a while. That is the only reason why I came to Hamburg. If Monica Seles had not played during these few days in Hamburg, I would have gone to the French Open in Paris to carry out my plan. At first today I sat quite high up in the center court. Later I sat in row 9 at seat 11. I was constantly wondering how I could get to Monica Seles. Today I already had the knife in a green

shopping bag. There was also a program in the bag. That was to hide the knife better. During those three days I constantly planned and tried out the various possibilities. I considered running directly out onto the center court to do it. But I was afraid of slipping because I had never been on a tennis court and I did not know whether I could run on it with normal shoes. Anyway, there were too many people standing there who might have prevented me. Today I noticed how relatively easy it is to walk along the first row and get behind Monica Seles. I had already thought through various means of getting to Seles. I was present during her early morning training sessions; I also thought of the possibility of giving Monica a bunch of flowers. I also thought about the possibility of doing something of the kind while asking for an autograph.

"But finally I came to the decision to do it right there on center court. As I have already said, I used the break in play at 4 to 3 in the second set. I got up from my seat in row 9 and went off to the right. Then I went down the stairs to the first row and turned left directly along the side of the court toward the umpire. The break in play usually lasts about a minute, so I had to move relatively quickly. When I was standing directly behind Monica Seles I put my right hand into the shopping bag, let it drop, and then grabbed the knife with both hands. I then turned to the right and stabbed Monica Seles from about shoulder height. I could only see the top part of her back as she was sitting on the bench. I did not stab her with all my strength, because I only wanted to injure her. I don't know whether I intended to hit a certain part of her body. There were so many people standing about that I had to act quickly. Besides, the minute was almost over and Monica Seles would then have stood up. Because of the point the match was at, it was possible that she might not have sat down again. Straight after stabbing her I was overpowered by people . . .

"This act was her punishment for the past three years. It really upset me that Monica Seles was above Steffi Graf in the world tennis ranking. I think I will probably get fifteen years' imprisonment. When I get out of prison Steffi Graf will obviously no longer be playing tennis. I would not repeat such an act. For me, it is now over and done with. It was just her punishment *for the past three years. Originally I had intended to send a letter to Stephanie's mother beforehand, informing her that I intended to take action. But I didn't do so, so that nothing would point to me intending to do such an act . . .*

"I am not certain, but I cannot remember yelling as I stabbed her. Nor do I know anything of Monica Seles screaming. It all happened very quickly and I was very happy to have made it that far.

"On being asked again, I emphasize once more that I did not want to kill Monica Seles. My sole aim was to injure her in such a way that she would not be able to play tennis for a while. I wanted to help Stephanie. I see the whole thing as a warning — to Monica Seles's parents as well. After I had stabbed her some people shouted out that I was a pig. And yet I did it for the spectators as well. I was a bit confused by the reaction of the spectators."

4

Less than a week after Günther Parche attempted to end my tennis career and quite possibly my life, the Women's Tennis Association voted on the state of my ranking. The head of the WTA, Gerard Smith, met in Rome with seventeen of the top twenty-five players on the tour. He asked them to vote on whether or not to freeze my rank while I recuperated from the attack. The result was a "near-unanimous" vote against any protection of my ranking. I was told that all the top players were in agreement, with the exception of Gabriela Sabatini, who abstained from the vote. My ranking would not be protected, which meant that Steffi Graf could regain the number one position with a win at the 1993 French Open. I was devastated.

My manager, Stephanie Tolleson, said it best: "What upsets Monica the most isn't the ranking as much as the way she's losing it. This guy set out to hurt her and her ranking, and now he seems to have accomplished the sick thing he was after. Certainly it has to be bittersweet for Graf to become number one in this way." Stephanie added that there was a general public perception that ranking should be won on the tennis court, not by a knife.

I was very surprised at the WTA decision. I believed that the players would have thought more about humanity than their rankings. I have always had respect for my opponents — for their skills, strategies, spirits, and for all the hard work they've put in to achieve their respective rankings. That vote showed me that the respect I felt for them was not returned.

I was disappointed to learn that Steffi Graf had also agreed my ranking

16

shouldn't be protected. Steffi and I had cried together in my hospital room in Hamburg. I believed that she'd be on my side, if only for a moment; that she wouldn't want to become number one as the result of a deranged fan's actions.

When asked by the press about ranking after the vote, Steffi stated, "I'm not even thinking about that. Knowing the guy was one of my fans, that's been difficult."

What amazed me most was that the media never picked up on the vote. They never recognized that all but one of the top players wanted to knock me out of the game. By 1993 I was winning every major tournament in the world. I was at the top of my game — feeling comfortable and confident. With me out of the way, the path would be clear for other players — especially those within reach of the top five positions.

Those players saw a chance to move up in rankings, and they didn't seem to care that another human being had been stabbed for that opportunity. Rank doesn't mean anything, at least not by itself. But couple rank with endorsements, bonuses from sponsors, and millions of dollars are at stake. My lawyers have told me that in the year following the attack I lost an estimated ten million dollars in income. In addition, contracts that would have gone to me went to other players.

Megadollars mean something to everyone. There are players whose incomes went up literally by millions after the attack in Hamburg. Suddenly, rank meant a lot. And you can bet that those players who moved up, who moved closer to number one than ever before, would have preferred me not to return to the tour.

5

A few days after my attack in Hamburg I knew several things. My attacker's name was Günther Parche. He stabbed me because he was a fan of Steffi Graf's and I stood between her and the number one ranking. Second, the Citizen Cup had continued, despite the attack. Third, only four days after the attack the top women players on the tour had almost unanimously voted not to honor my ranking while I recuperated. I had been the top female tennis player in the world, but there was no consideration given to my position.

I lay in my hospital bed thinking: Günther Parche got just what he wanted. Steffi Graf will be number one in a few weeks, and I'm out of the game. I couldn't think further than that; couldn't wonder if the police would believe Parche's statement, that his "sole aim was to injure [me] in such a way that [I] would not be able to play tennis for a while." The statement was too ridiculous to even consider. The only reason Parche's knife hadn't gone straight into my spine, according to my doctors, was that he'd been off by a few millimeters. The only reason it hadn't gone deeper was that I'd leaned forward to towel off my face at the exact moment of his thrust. The only reason he hadn't killed me was that he was stopped by a security guard as he raised his arms to stab again.

"I just want to go home," I told my family between tears. I had been in the hospital in Hamburg for two nights. The doctors were running blood tests and keeping an eye on my wound. Over two days, I was given countless shots to combat infections. "I want to go home," I said on Sunday morning. Stephanie Tolleson took control.

Within hours, I was transported by ambulance to a private medical plane, complete with a doctor and nurse. The plane was too small to take Stephanie and my parents, so Zoltan flew with me. I felt like an empty shell as I lay on the small bed in the plane. I just wanted to go somewhere beautiful and peaceful, where I trusted the doctors and where I was surrounded by my family.

The plane ride was a long one. There was no bathroom on the plane, and we had to stop twice to refuel and to use the restrooms. Almost twenty hours later the plane landed in Denver, Colorado.

"Only a few more hours," Zoltan said with a smile as I was loaded into another ambulance.

I tried to think about Vail, and the Steadman Hawkins clinic. I'd been there before for a shin injury in 1991. I liked Dr. Steadman and Dr. Hawkins. They are the top knee and shoulder orthopedic surgeons (respectively) in the country, and great human beings whom I trusted.

In the ambulance on the way to Vail I tried to let go of my obsessive thoughts about Parche; tried not to see his face, hear my scream, smell the shirt and see the blood-caked knife. They're going to lock him up and throw away the key, I thought. Parche himself said that he expected fifteen years in prison. So focus on recovering from this — that's what's important now. Little did I know then that one more certainty in my life would be shattered — my faith in the judicial system.

Dr. Richard Steadman and Dr. Richard Hawkins weren't at the clinic when I arrived. Both had been out of Colorado over the weekend. When Stephanie told them that I'd be coming to Vail, they changed their plans and made reservations to return to Vail on Monday. I was met by John Atkins, a great physical therapist who has worked with countless top athletes. He got my brother and me settled into our suite. At that point, I still couldn't sleep without Zoltan or another family member present.

Topper Hagerman also stopped by to make sure I was comfortable. He's another super physical therapist at the clinic. I remember I couldn't stop crying: the nicer they were, the more I cried. And I was talking through the tears, but making no sense at all. Really irrational stuff came out of my mouth. I heard it, and I knew I was babbling, but I couldn't seem to stop. I was confused, in a state of shock, and emotionally and physically spent.

That night I couldn't sleep. The pain was terrible and my emotions raw. I kept seeing Parche's face, kept hearing my scream. Over and over again, the face and the scream. I felt as if I was losing my mind. When sleep crept up on me and began to steal my consciousness, I'd fight it.

"I can't go to sleep," I told my brother. "If I do, he'll come . . . someone wants to kill me, Zoltan. Don't let him, okay?"

Without my brother, I don't know how I would have made it through the first few nights in Vail. If he hadn't been at the stadium in Hamburg, I can't imagine how I would have survived. Zoltan consistently took my focus off the attack — in the first few minutes, in the hospital, and in Vail. "Help me," I cried repeatedly to Zoltan over the next few weeks. And he did, because he's my big brother and he loves me.

I saw Dr. Hawkins first. On Monday morning he cleaned my wound and began to assess the damage to my tissues and muscles. He believed I'd need at least a month of rehabilitation before we could assess how the wound would affect my game. That afternoon I saw Dr. Steadman. He also checked my wound, and then we began to talk about my rehabilitation. For the first few weeks I'd need to keep my shoulder inactive. Other than light massage and stretching, I wouldn't work my arm. After that, we'd see.

My parents arrived that night. We spent a quiet evening until I received a call from Stephanie Tolleson. "You've got to hold a press conference," she told me. "If you don't the press will flock down to Vail. It'll be the same as 1991 — speculations and untrue stories."

I agreed. That year I'd pulled out of Wimbledon because of shin splints but hadn't given a statement to the press. The result had been a month-long tabloid frenzy. I wouldn't make that mistake again.

The following morning Dr. Steadman, Dr. Hawkins, Bob Kain (the head of the tennis division at IMG) and I held a press conference —

the second big conference of my life. (The first was after Wimbledon '91, when an overzealous promoter created a circus before my first match after withdrawing from Wimbledon.)

There were hundreds of reporters in Vail. The conference was live, so there were television crews as well. I remember looking out at all the people and feeling scared. For the most part, the journalists were kind. They never asked me about Parche, or what I thought would happen to him. I guess they figured that since 10,000 people had seen the attack, the guy would go to jail. End of story. The press conference went by in a blur — I was still in shock, and while my body was at the conference, my mind was focused on the attack. I remember only one specific question. A reporter asked me to take off my shirt to show the media my stab wound. Bob Kain quickly spoke up and helped me to extricate myself from that uncomfortable situation gracefully. I wasn't alone in thinking that the question had been rude.

That afternoon I went back to see Dr. Steadman. Dad came with me. He still wasn't feeling too well, and now the altitude in Vail was affecting his breathing. Dr. Steadman looked over at him — his face was pale and he was sweating a bit. "Maybe you should see an internist in Vail, Mr. Seles," he suggested. "Just get a little blood work done." My dad tried to joke about how he felt, but Dr. Steadman insisted.

While my father visited an internist, Mom, Zoltan and I paced around Vail. So strange, I thought dully. A few days ago I was thinking about Wimbledon, that maybe this year I could win it, go all the way. Now I can't lift my arm. We met my father after his appointment. I knew something was wrong the moment I looked at him.

"No big deal," he said as we drove the next morning to see a doctor in Denver. "The internist just thinks I should visit another doctor."

We sat in the waiting room while my father was examined. Then a nurse appeared and ushered us all into an inner office.

"Mr. Seles," the doctor said when he saw me enter the room, "do you think Monica should be here? She's already under great shock."

"My daughter has always known everything about me. I cannot lie

21

to her. It wouldn't be fair. Sooner or later she'd find out," Dad said with a weak smile.

My stomach began to churn, and I sank slowly into a chair.

"Mrs. Seles," the doctor said to my mom, "there's no easy way to say this. Your husband has prostate cancer. The good news is that we've caught it early. The bad news is that he needs immediate surgery."

Cancer? The word had never entered my mind. I'd been prepared for trouble with Dad's heart, maybe his kidneys. But cancer? That word was like *stabbed* — it had never been a part of my vocabulary.

"I can schedule him for surgery and treatment at the Mayo Clinic this Friday," the doctor continued.

"Wait, wait, wait" my father interrupted. "This is all going too fast. Let us think about this."

"Mr. Seles, prostate cancer is serious. It can be deadly. Don't think too long," the doctor said sternly.

We drove back to Vail in silence. When we got to the room we called Mark McCormack, CEO and founder of International Management Group, for advice. He suggested that my father should see a particular physician — Dr. Ian Hay — at the Mayo Clinic for a second opinion; if it was prostate cancer he should do what the doctor advised.

My father flew to Rochester, Minnesota, the following Monday. Zoltan accompanied him because Dad's English wasn't great. My mother stayed with me.

Cancer. That word raced through my mind. In my native country, if a doctor said someone had cancer, they were dead. Why are these things happening? I wondered. Why does my dad have to deal with all this stuff right now, when I need him here with me?

My dad called from the clinic the following day. "Well, I'm going to have to have the surgery."

"We'll be there when you get out of the operation," my mother said softly. We packed our bags and headed for Rochester.

Seeing my father in the hospital, so soon after I'd been the one in the bed, was terrible. First of all, dads are supposed to always be strong and healthy. At nineteen, I found it very strange to think that my father might be sick. I began to cry when I entered his room. He tried to be upbeat for me, but I said, "Dad, you don't have to do that, I know how you feel."

"Don't worry, Monica," my father said with a weak smile, "I won't die, because cancer is my friend." Even in his fear and pain, he tried to make the situation better for me.

The operation had been a success, but the doctors told us they wouldn't know if the cancer was gone for a year. During that time my dad would receive mild doses of chemotherapy.

I stayed with my father until he was ready to leave the hospital. Then I returned to Vail with my mother to continue therapy. As the days progressed, I grew more and more distant. Life wasn't what I'd bargained for all those years ago as a child. Back then, all I'd seen were limitless possibilities. There were no monsters, except in my dreams, and the future was a golden point on the distant horizon.

6

Zoltan was the one who saw Bjorn Borg play on our television and told my father he wanted to play. A week after Zoltan said he wanted to be a tennis player, my father got him a racket. There were no racket stores in our hometown so my dad drove ten hours to Italy. He brought Zoltan back a racket and a T-shirt like the one Borg had worn in tournaments.

My father knew nothing about tennis. He'd been a physical education major in college and a top triple jumper, so he understood sports, the body, and biomechanics. But tennis? Nobody played tennis in our family. My father went to every bookstore he could find in our town. Finally, he came across an old paperback book on the game. From reading that book, and using his understanding of athletics, my dad taught Zoltan how to play.

What about me? Zoltan was fourteen, eight years older than me. He was my big brother, and I wanted to be just like him. The story goes that one afternoon my brother was lifting a heavy weight before he went out to practice with my dad. I walked over and picked up one of the weights and began lifting.

My dad was in shock. "What is this, Monica?" he said as he raced over to take the weight out of my hand. "It is too heavy for you, little one," he explained.

But the incredible thing was that it wasn't too heavy. I had unbelievable strength for a little girl.

It was the same with bottle tops. In our town the soda pop bottles had tops that were so difficult to open that neither my parents nor my brother could manage them. At the age of five years, I could pop the tops off with one hand. That's when my father began to realize that I had more than just a strong grip.

"I want to play tennis, too," I announced.

"Why not?" my father grinned. He knew I was strong enough to hold the racket. He got in the car, drove to Italy, and picked up a tiny wooden racket.

"Here you go, Monica," he said as he handed me my new racket. I grabbed it with both hands and swung like I'd seen my brother swing. Except that I didn't let go with either hand — forehand or backhand.

"That's not the way to hold it," Zoltan tried to explain.

"Looks natural that way," my father commented. "Monica, if it feels right, hold the racket in both hands."

From that moment on, I was rarely separated from my racket. I even slept with it on my pillow. And every morning before school, I'd go out to the brick wall of our apartment building and hit against it for an hour. None of the neighbors complained. Here was a little girl making a noise hitting against the wall at 6:00 am, and they thought it was cute! After school, I'd return to the wall and hit for a few more hours.

There were very few tennis courts in our town. It was difficult to get on them, so my father, brother, and I played in the parking lot of our apartment building. We strung a net between rows of cars, and hit down the narrow court. The uneven surface made the ball bounce strangely, and we spent a lot of time crawling beneath cars to find our balls, but those practices and games were a lot of fun.

I think about that sometimes — learning to play in a parking lot: stringing nets between cars, hopping up on bumpers to reach shots. I learned to play by hitting against a brick wall, not a ball machine or other players. And my father was my coach — teaching me from a twenty-year-old book, and a new system he developed. I was lucky my dad was so creative and capable. When I hear people say that you can't make it in tennis if you don't have a lot of money, I know they're wrong. We lived in a socialist country, and we didn't have much money. But I loved the sport, and that was enough.

"Papa Seles is crazy. He shouldn't make his little girl play tennis, and she shouldn't be holding the racket with two hands on both sides, either." That's what a lot of people in our town said about my dad the first year I played. "Girls shouldn't play tennis — she'll never make it."

My dad smiled at people when they said those things. It took a lot of strength not to let them bother him, but he succeeded because he believed in me and I believed in him. Every day I dragged him out to our makeshift court, begging him to hit balls with me and teach me. And because Dad had so much energy, he learned to play tennis right along with me.

My father never made me play; but hour after hour, days, months, years, I made him. I was a child, and I didn't care if he was bone tired after work, if he wanted to sleep in on a Saturday: I wanted to play tennis.

I think one of the reasons my father has always been so supportive of his children's aims is that his family never understood his. My dad was an only child. His parents were farmers, and his father wanted him to become a farmer, too. But when he went to college, he decided to study physical education. His parents didn't understand that, or why he eventually chose to be a cartoonist. They loved him, but they didn't understand. That's why, when my father saw his children's passion for tennis, he wanted to support us.

My father's mother was one of the biggest critics of my tennis. "She should be playing with dolls and her friends," she used to say. "It's not normal for a little girl."

"Grandma, I love to play tennis," I'd explain. My mother, at that point, sided with my grandmother.

"Maybe, Monica, you are spending a little too much time on the tennis court," she said. But eventually she gave up trying to change me. "It is her personality to play, and as long as she is smiling and happy . . ." she finally said to my grandmother with a shrug.

Within a year of picking up a racket, my brother was winning every tournament he entered and was a top ranked junior player in Europe.

Dad had focused on Zoltan's technique, and his expertise had paid off. He began to help me with mine. A six-year-old child cannot understand biomechanics: my father knew I wouldn't get the physics of why and how to hit a ball, so he devised a way to help me understand.

My dad is a cartoonist and artist. He did a children's television program that ran every weekend, teaching kids how to paint and do crafts. In addition, he sold his cartoons to newspapers around the world. And for me, he drew to help me to play tennis.

There was "little Mo." Little Mo was a cartoon rabbit that my father drew on a thick booklet of paper. When I flipped through the pages quickly, Mo came to life. Dad used the rabbit to demonstrate things like serving technique. For example, if I was leaning too far back, or my behind was sticking out, he'd draw Mo serving that way. Then he'd draw a correct version so that I could see the difference. Not only did it work; it eliminated frustration. Every time I played, I saw improvement.

Dad didn't just understand biomechanics. He had a talent for knowing when I was imitating, instead of drawing on my natural skills. In the beginning I used to serve like John McEnroe when he was in his prime. He had this exaggerated swing: he'd turn completely sideways at the baseline, which is very unusual. John is the only player who ever did that, but I liked his serve so I copied it. Eventually, the motion started to strain my knee. My father changed my serve until the movement was painless and fluid. He found my natural swing, not an imitation.

Dad always had an innate talent for coaching tennis. He can visualize the way a stroke should be, and he can get that across to me. He didn't just use cartoons to help me. He devised different drills that not only helped my game, but kept me from getting bored. I liked to play small tennis. We used to stand at the T-line and play entire sets. I learned control and placement that way.

I played in my first tournament when I was six and a half years old. I came in third and won a trophy. At that point I didn't know how to score and had to wait for the umpire to tell me when the match was over! Later, when I became a professional tennis player, I'd miss those shiny silver and gold trophies I received in junior tournaments. Enormous paper checks or crystal bowls just didn't feel quite the same. Neither did practices.

My favorite cartoon was Tom and Jerry. In practice, Dad would draw the mouse on my tennis balls, and then take his thick black marker and draw the cat on my T-shirt. I'd chase after the balls as if I was Tom and each one was Jerry. If I caught Jerry a certain number of times, I'd get a prize. Dad would also make bets with me — if I did ten good serves he'd get a beer, and I'd get an ice cream. Even if I didn't manage ten serves, I'd still get the ice cream.

By the time I was eight years old, I was the number one junior player in Yugoslavia. Within a few years, I was the best junior player in the world — traveling to different countries and loving every minute of my life.

7

When I first began to play tennis, it seemed that my town of Novi Sad was the perfect place for the game. There was the brick wall of my apartment building and a makeshift tennis court between cars in the parking lot. But as I got better and better, my father began to realize that these facilities would eventually limit my progress. I needed to be on a tennis court every day, and I needed to play on different surfaces.

Four. That's the number of tennis courts we had in our town when I was a kid. Tennis was not a big sport there, but it was still difficult for a young child to get much court time. Add to that the fact that they were all clay courts, which meant that, whenever I went to a tournament on supreme or hard, I was at a great disadvantage. And there was one more problem: none of the courts was indoors and winters were freezing. It's impossible to play in snow and ice-cold rain — it isn't good to the body, not to mention the balls. During the long winters I practiced on indoor walls and volleyball courts.

Luckily I'd begun winning a lot of junior tournaments, and my father and I were traveling to the United States several times a year for tournaments like Sport Goofy in DisneyWorld, Florida. It was in Florida, during an Orange Bowl match, that I first met Nick Bollettieri.

"How would you like to come train at my tennis academy for a few weeks?" Nick asked. I was uncertain. I'd heard about the Bollettieri Academy in Bradenton, Florida, but my family didn't have much money and I knew we couldn't afford it. "Just come see if you like the academy," Nick offered. "If you do, maybe you can come train."

"Why not, Monica?" my father asked with a smile. It was a free two weeks playing in the warmth and sunshine.

The most amazing thing about the academy was that they had every type of court surface. You could literally play a few games on supreme court, then move outside to green clay or hard courts! My father and I spent two weeks practicing in the sun and heat, and I don't know whether I could have torn myself away from Florida if my grandmother hadn't died.

It wasn't until almost a year later, at a Miami tournament, that Nick approached our family again. By that time I was the number one junior player in the world and had won the world championship numerous times. I was also on my way to winning the Orange Bowl — comparable to the US Open for juniors. "We'd like to offer Monica a scholarship if she'd like it," Nick said.

"Sounds great!" my father said with a smile. "Let us think about it, and we'll get back to you."

"Would you like to train and go to school in Florida?" my father asked when we were alone.

"I guess it would be great for my tennis," I said with excitement. "But can you and Mom come, too?"

"No, Monica," Dad said. "You would have to go with your brother. Mom and I can't afford to come with you — we must keep our jobs."

"It's going to be great for my tennis," I said as emphatically as a thirteen-year-old can say anything. "Let's do it."

Zoltan moved into an academy apartment with me, and we fell into the rigid schedule of a tennis school. My brother began hitting with Andre Agassi, Jim Courier and David Wheaton. I worked with Zoltan, Nick, and the academy coaches. At first it was fun. There were a lot of kids, all from different parts of the US or abroad. Not all of us spoke the same language, but we could understand each other anyway. There were so many new things at that point — new coaches, tennis techniques, school classes — that I didn't have time to feel lonely. But once I sank into the schedule, I began to miss my parents. In addition, my game began to suffer.

One of the first things the academy coaches did was to change my swing from a two-fisted to a one-handed forehand. The ground strokes my father had spent years perfecting began to slide. I started to lose matches. The first was to a girl named Carrie Cunningham. Carrie was a year older than me, and I'd beaten her in the past. In 1987 she beat me 6–0, 6–1. "What is happening to me?" I asked in frustration after the match. I'd felt my game slipping, but until that match I hadn't realized how bad things were.

I didn't tell my parents anything was wrong. Each Saturday they'd call and I'd say that everything was okay, that I was fine, my game was strong, and I was doing well in school. I have always been the sort of person who tries to please other people more than myself. And, if I'm not trying to please, I'm hiding what I really think because I don't want anybody to feel sad for me.

I knew that my father couldn't leave his job. He was doing his children's television show and he was freelancing cartoons worldwide. It took both jobs plus my mother's wages from a computer job to take care of our family. I knew that my father felt that if he and Mom quit their work, they'd be putting a lot of pressure on me to succeed. He never wanted me to live with that type of financial pressure — especially at the age of thirteen.

But the truth was that I wasn't doing well. My game was deteriorating. And school? School was even worse. I had no idea what was going on in my classes. Literature, American history — I was struggling with English, so how could I understand them? Back home we learned the British way to speak and write, which is very proper. But in the US there was so much slang, so many different accents.

My brother spoke better English than I did, and he tried to help. He bought a notebook and every day he wrote down five new words. "Monica," he would say, "this is your homework. Every day learn these words and tomorrow I'll give you more." The only subject in school I did well in was math.

"You must come out here or I'm coming home," I finally broke down

31

and cried to my parents. I'd been at the academy for five months, and I couldn't take any more. I desperately missed my mom and dad — I was just a kid, lost in a country where I couldn't understand the language. The only reason I'd come to the academy was for my tennis game, and I was playing terribly.

"You come, or I go," I said miserably. At that point I didn't consider the fact that I was asking my parents to quit their jobs without any guarantee of an income. I didn't understand that they would have to leave their homeland, their parents, family and friends. I was unhappy, and I wanted them.

"Monica, it will put too much pressure on you," my mother tried to explain.

"Monica, we have to think about this," my father said. "It means leaving everything we've worked for all our lives. Everything."

They thought for a week, and then called me at the academy. "Well, we are going to take a leave of absence from our jobs for six months," my dad explained. "I'll try to do freelance cartoon work in Florida, and hopefully that'll pay our expenses." A few weeks later my parents arrived in Florida and moved into an apartment provided by the academy.

"Monica, what has happened!" my father asked the first day he watched me practice. "Zoltan!" he yelled across the court to my brother. "What did you let them do to her?" My style, my tennis grip, my two-handed forehand and backhand were all changed. "What you are born with — that is how you play," my father fumed. I had picked up the racket with two hands, therefore, he believed, I was meant to hit that way. "I am coach again," he told the academy coaches. "I'll work with my daughter."

We developed our own routine at the academy. Instead of playing every day but Sunday like the rest of the students, I took off two full days a week. My father and I believed that was good both physically and mentally. As a result, I was much fresher during practices, and more eager to play. In addition, if I woke up in the morning and felt tired, we didn't practice. "It's no good if you're not in the mood," Dad would say. We both always had a pretty light, common sense attitude towards practice. In the mornings and late afternoons we worked, and from 11:00 am until 3:00 pm I went to school. Although school was still difficult, I began to do better because I was happier.

There has always been a good balance in my home. My father is my coach on the court, but when we step off, he's my dad. And my mother? She never liked sports when she was in school. She didn't do well at them, and tried to avoid athletics. She was never too involved in the game; instead, we shop together, take long walks, design clothing, talk. That's what I mean about a balance. My parents were never tennis parents, even though my dad was my coach. In my family, win or lose, I was always Monica.

And my brother? Zoltan stayed at the academy as a player until 1986. It is the honest truth that he had twice as much tennis talent as I did, but he had so much talent that he never felt he had to work, and as a result he slowly wandered away from tennis. I don't know why one of us was more focused than the other. I had the fire in my belly — I was born with it there. That's just the way it happened and my parents always loved us for who we were, not for what we might become.

That was not the case with all the parents at the academy. Some would yell at their kids during practices. "Stay on that court and practice three more hours!" they'd shout when their child lost a match. "How could you play so badly?"

I never understood those parents. During my years at the academy I saw kids who were big hopes but never materialized into great players. Basically, there were two kinds of parents at the academy — the ones who wanted to win more than their children, and the others who were supportive regardless of wins or losses.

I was one of the lucky ones. My family provided love and a nurturing environment. By the time 1987 ended, I was back on track. With tennis, school and, most importantly, my life. The future contained infinite possibilities — I was ready to join the tour as an amateur and play my first professional match.

8

They were there. That's what I remember more than anything else about my first professional tennis match in 1988. I was still an amateur — only fourteen years old. The match was a Virginia Slims in Boca Raton, Florida, and I was playing in the first round against Helen Kelesi. Whoever won the match would play Chris Evert next. At the time, Chris was the number three player in the world.

The only two women tennis players I watched as a child were Martina Navratilova and Chris. We didn't have many television stations back home, and when women's matches were televised, it was usually the finals. For years I thought those two were the only women in tennis.

The match against Kelesi was a tough one. I was nervous: nervous because we were playing on stadium court; nervous because Helen was a good player and I had to fight to win the first set, 7–6; and most of all, nervous because, in the second set, Chris Evert quietly entered the stadium and sat in the stands right across from me. We're 4 all in the second set, and Chris Evert is there, not to watch the match, but to watch me.

I tried to concentrate. That's when I saw Steffi Graf sit down in the stands. I hadn't seen Steffi in person for years. We both competed in European championships when we were kids. Steffi was older, so I didn't play with her, but I remember seeing her on the courts — a tall, skinny girl who later grew up into a great champion. A champion who was now sitting in the stands watching me play! A few minutes later Gabriela Sabatini also appeared to watch the match.

Up until the moment I saw Chris, Steffi, and Gaby, I was just a young kid who some considered a big hopeful. The only other time in my life when I've been more distracted than I was that sunny afternoon was my first appearance at Wimbledon, when I couldn't take my eyes off Princess Diana. I ran forward to shake Helen's hand after winning the match in two sets. I'm going to play Chris Evert tomorrow, I thought in amazement.

"Second round: Chris Evert vs. Monica Seles." Just to read those words on the program — wow! I remember walking from the locker room to stadium court. It was night and the court lights made the entire scene seem surreal. This is not a dream, I told myself. I'm walking next to Chris Evert . . . I'm about to play a match against Chris.

It was a pretty long match. Most games went to deuce, but when it came to winning, Chris usually closed me out. I played well, but my knees shook most of the game. Chris beat me in two sets, 6–2, 6–1, but I was happy with my performance. The thing I remember most about the match was that a big brown insect, probably drawn by the powerful tennis lights, landed by my feet. I picked the guy up and took him to the sidelines so he wouldn't get crushed. It was the fluttering of the brown insect in my cupped hands that reminded me that the match wasn't a dream.

Five days later I went down to Key Biscayne for a tournament. I won my first match fairly easily against an Australian girl named Louise Field.

After the match Andre Agassi came down to the side of the court to congratulate me for playing well. I knew Andre from the academy, and he'd always been really nice to me.

After my match with Louise, I returned to the locker room. I thought that if the press wanted to talk to me, someone would get me and take me to the post-match press conference. Well, that's not the way it works. After every match players are required to go to a press conference. The tournament's publicist found me changing in the locker room. "You're supposed to be with the press," she explained. I wasn't fined that time, because I was an amateur, but the publicist sat me down and explained what the Women's Tennis Association required from all its players.

The following night I played Gabriela Sabatini. It was overwhelming enough that Gaby was ranked number four in the world, but in addition, the crowd was in her court. This was the first match I'd played where the positive energy of the spectators was clearly focused on my opponent. The crowd was largely Hispanic, and they love Gaby down there. As I stepped out on to the court I thought, I'm going to go out there and not be as nervous as I was with Chris. That was my only goal.

I played out of my mind for the first five games. I was up 4–1, and my head was dizzy with the idea that I might actually win the first set. I became so nervous that I couldn't play for a few games. By the time I came back down to earth, Gaby had won the first set, 7–6. That's a pretty bad feeling — being up by so much and then, in what feels like seconds, losing the set. Worse still, you have to win the next two sets to take the match. It's not fun.

If I blow the first set, I get pretty angry. Then I start playing without inhibitions. Regardless of whether it's nerves, or lack of concentration, I just try to let go of my fears and play all out — like I do in practice.

I've never been able to play during a match as well as I play in practice. In practice there are no inhibitions, no nerves, no line people to disagree with, no calls that rattle your focus. When I'm down in a match as a result of my own mental state, I try to summon up the same attitude I have in practices. Sometimes it works for me, but in that match against Gaby it didn't. I lost in two sets and was out of the tournament in the second round.

Not that it mattered. I was an amateur, playing with no expectations. In 1987 winning against the top ten players wasn't even in my mind. I was content to play great games. The idea that I might get a set off someone like Gaby or Chris was satisfying enough.

"When are you going to turn pro?" The question first started popping up after I played well against Chris and Gaby. I wasn't in any rush. I knew that I was very young. When you're fourteen there's no guarantee that a tennis career will work out. There's no guarantee at twenty-one for that matter. But I knew that if I chose to end my sports career as an amateur, I'd still have the opportunity to go to college on a scholarship. Once I went professional, there would be no scholarship.

There were drawbacks, of course, to remaining amateur. Amateurs don't get prize money. If they win a tournament they get a small percentage of the prize to pay for their hotels, airlines, food. The rules are strict, and exact receipts have to be kept. Still, college was enough to keep me from grabbing what might have been a brass and not a golden ring.

Just remember what's important, I reminded myself for the next year. My family — our health and well-being — and the future were my top priorities. Those values didn't change when I finally decided to go professional in February of 1989. That's when the reality of tennis as big business, not just a game, became clear.

9

"I'm fifteen years old, and I'm sorry, but I'm not going to play on a hurt ankle." That's what I told the Virginia Slims tournament organizers in Washington, DC, in February of 1989. "I want to play, but I'm sorry, you guys, I can't — it's not worth it."

Of course I wanted to play. It was my first tournament as a professional and I'd just beaten Manuela Maleeva in the quarterfinals. Manuela was ranked number nine in the world. I was ranked eighty-eighth. The match had been a tough one, and I'd sprained my ankle in the second set. It was my first sprain (since then I've become an expert in sprained ankles), and while the pain was considerable, I decided I'd finish the match. I just told myself, it's hurting me, okay; I can still do this. I have two games left, and I'm going to do this.

I've always had a strong mind, but if Manuela had fought back and won the second set, I would have had to default before playing a third. Manuela was a back-court player who could hit forever. There was no way my ankle could have handled another complete set. Luckily, I won the next two games and the match.

It was an upset. Whenever a top ten player is beaten by someone ranked eighty-eighth in the world, it's an upset. The funny thing was, I was so proud to be ranked eighty-eighth after only three tournaments. I was the only player at the time to be ranked so high after so few matches. And I was ready for the semifinals against Zina Garrison. Zina was ranked sixth in the world, and I really wanted to play her. But my ankle wasn't up to another match.

I had to default. The tournament directors were pretty upset. With my default they lost their night match, and had to put on an exhibition. That meant they lost money, maybe sponsors. Tennis is big business, and the tournament directors had to answer to many pressures from different people. But the bottom line was that I was hurt. And if I played injured, I wouldn't have played well, and no one would have watched the match anyway. Still, I was disappointed — I had badly wanted to play.

It's very hard to default in a tournament, especially if you've been playing well. Any competitive athlete wants to go out on their playing field and show the world and themselves that they've got something special. But at fifteen, I wasn't willing to risk an injury that would affect my future in the game. I left DC with an ice pack on my ankle and a feeling of disappointment. Still, I was determined to nurse my ankle and return to the tour as soon as it was healed.

Old wounds don't heal very well, and that's what Carrie Cunningham was. In April 1989 I went to play in the Virginia Slims tournament in Houston. I moved through the first few rounds pretty easily, but was scheduled to play Carrie Cunningham in the semifinals. As I've said, Carrie and I had a history.

Long before I moved to the United States, I'd played against Carrie in the Disney Sport Goofy Tournament. I'd beaten her fairly easily, and always considered her a good player, but I knew I was better. Then, after living for several months at Nick Bollettieri's tennis academy, I played Carrie again. This time she beat me, 6–1, 6–0. I was devastated. The loss came at a time when I was questioning my decision to live at the academy, missing my parents, and wondering if I could be a top player without my father's coaching skills. And now, two years after that match, I had to play Carrie again.

To this day, I try not to think about my opponent's game. I just go out on the court and play mine, to my best ability. I don't focus on someone's weak backhand, strong volleys, or cross-court drives, just on my own strengths and weaknesses. I don't watch videos of matches, either. If you want to see my hair stand on end, tell me to watch a video! I beat Carrie Cunningham, 6–0, 6–1. It was a relief, and a big confidence boost. I needed that confidence because I had to play Chris in the finals.

I had no sponsors in 1989. No one sent me new tennis skirts or fancy sneakers to wear. But I wanted to look good for my match with Chris, so I went to a booth at the tournament and spoke with the owner about getting a special shirt for my match. "Sure," he said, "come on over tonight after the store closes and we'll pick out something."

The next day I showed up on court in a new shirt: it had no logos or patches. As I stood at the net before the match, a photographer asked, "May I take a picture of you?" Wow, I thought with growing excitement; a high publicity match against Chris. All I wanted to do was play well. I looked over at Chris, so cool and controlled, and felt a buzz in my stomach. It was time to play.

I lost the first set, 6–3. My only thought was that I'd won one more game than the last time we played. I just told myself to enjoy the second set; to go out there and lose my inhibitions, forget about who I was playing, and just play my game like I'd done in practice. I won the second set, 6–1.

I took a set from Chris Evert, I repeated in my head as we began the third set. Before I knew it, I was up, 5–3. Chris hit me a pretty easy ball, and I remember thinking: Oh my God, I'm going to win this match and beat Chris. A zillion thoughts raced through my mind as the ball came toward me — I saw Chris . . . I saw the ball . . . heard the crowd . . . tried to concentrate . . . hit a winner. And then it was over and I'd closed the match, 6–4.

Many players say that when they win, the world goes into slow motion. It's just the opposite for me. It's as if someone had pulled the plug out of the universe, and everything slides together so quickly that it's hard to comprehend. Chris was saying, "Great match," as we shook hands. My father was cheering and I was hugging him (my mother had been unable to make the trip because her father was ill). The tournament directors were handing me an oversized check for more money than I'd ever thought of earning. I was thanking my family and friends. And then I was alone in the locker room.

"Where's the trophy?" I shyly asked someone who worked for the tournament.

"There are no trophies, Monica. The check is the trophy," the man replied.

"Oh," I said sadly. I had really wanted a trophy. "Can I keep the big check?" I asked. The man nodded with a smile.

That night my father and I flew back to Florida. I carried that enormous green cardboard check on the plane with me. A lot of the passengers asked what the check was, and I told them I'd just won my first professional tournament. I can still remember the feeling — something great was inside me and kept bubbling up. Now I get a check and think, good, and then move on to the next tournament.

A week after the Houston match a trophy arrived in the mail. The tournament director had had it specially made for me! It was a very sweet gesture. Meanwhile, I went back to my practice regimen. Neither my father nor I dwelled on the match. He had been thrilled at my victory, but the tournament was over. In my family we don't make a big or a small deal of each match. And we never make much of the money, either. Even though we didn't have a lot back home, it was never a goal. I have always understood that it couldn't buy the important things in life.

10

I wanted it more than anything I'd ever wanted in my seven years on earth. Red and yellow and cream colored — no doubt in my mind, it was the most beautiful thick soft cotton comforter and pillow set I'd ever seen. Each cost as much money as my mother made in a month, but we still went down to the department store in Novi Sad to look.

"Well, Monica, they're really expensive," my mom said slowly.

"Maybe I can do some job to earn the money for them," I said hopefully. It might take three or four years, but it'll be worth it, I thought.

"Your birthday and Christmas are coming up," she finally said. "If you really want both, we'll get them as a combined present."

I wanted that comforter and pillow so badly. The word *yes* was on the tip of my tongue. But I remember it didn't taste right. "How about just the comforter," I said in a voice I hoped wouldn't betray the torn feeling I had inside. My mom smiled. Even as a kid, I always paid attention to the price tag.

When I was seven years old, I already understood money. I knew what it was to have it, and that having some didn't mean you had enough. Money was always an issue because of the extensive traveling I needed to do for tennis. When I traveled outside of Yugoslavia our money didn't go as far because of the exchange rate. I recall booking airline tickets for tournaments because I spoke better English than my parents. At eight, nine, ten years old, I struggled to find the cheapest fares, the least expensive hotel rooms. I wasn't being frugal — it was the only way I could have played tennis.

When I began to make money, things didn't change much. If you've had to struggle to make ends meet, and then you begin to have money, there are two ways to go. Some people get extravagant: they buy sports cars for themselves and their friends; they go on expensive trips, purchase jewelry. I never did that. Maybe it's because money was never the object. Playing good tennis was the goal.

I'm not saying that the money that came along with winning wasn't welcomed. Being a professional tennis player is like running a small business. There are a lot of expenses — travel, hitting partners, physical therapists, coaches, hotels. Unlike team sports, expenses are sizable and are left to the individual. In addition to supporting my career, money has given my family security, a beautiful home and a lot of freedom. But it has always been a means to an end, a way to support the family that had supported me, with no guarantees. My parents had given up their homeland, their livelihoods, their family and friends, so that I could play tennis. There was no promise that I'd earn money in the game when, at thirteen, I went to train at the Bollettieri Academy.

Only you can let money change your life. That's what my parents always believed. When I began to bring home $200,000 checks, nothing important changed in my household. I didn't go out and buy a Ferrari — in fact, the first nice car I ever bought myself was a Ford Explorer, and I bought it in 1995. It's true that I had record career earnings in '91 and '92, and signed some lucrative endorsement contracts. But through it all, my parents' warnings have stayed in my ears. "Monica, remember that money comes and goes," my parents said. "You've got to be the same person regardless of whether or not you have it. Keep your feet always on the ground where they belong."

After the attack in 1993 I didn't earn any money for two years. And though there were rumors that I collected insurance money, they were untrue. I didn't collect a penny. Some of my sponsors believed in me and kept me on; some dropped me; and one decided to sue me for staying out of the game. During that year I realized more than ever that my parents had been right — that there was no guarantee I'd continue to earn money playing tennis. And the person I was, the family and friends I had, the life I'd chosen, were the only things that truly belonged to me.

I still have that cotton comforter from when I was seven. It's old now — the colors are faded and some of the stitching has ripped apart. But when I look at it, I don't see the soda stain, or the unraveling edges; I see the beautiful comforter I wanted more than anything when I was seven years old. I remember what it was like when money wasn't so plentiful, when birthday and holiday presents had to be combined. And I smile, because none of the important stuff has changed.

11

The important things never changed, but by 1989 I was growing up. Part of that meant mildly rebelling against my mother's wishes.

"Please, Zoltan . . . please," I begged.

"Mom said not until you're eighteen," my brother replied.

"Come on . . . please," I wheedled. My mother had forbidden me to dye my hair blonde before the 1989 French Open. It was my first Grand Slam event, and I was determined to look special for it!

"You're only fifteen years old, Monica," Mom had explained. "When you're eighteen you can do whatever you want."

"But I want to be a blonde," I'd tried to explain.

"You'll just have to wait," she replied before flying back to Yugoslavia to visit her father.

Mom would never have given in, but Zoltan did, and I arrived at the French Open with strawberry-blonde hair and some of the most unique tennis outfits ever worn for a Grand Slam.

When I was a kid I loved to create costumes for my Barbie dolls and teddy bears. I had a bureau filled with small dresses. So naturally when I began to compete in professional tennis I wanted to design my own outfits. Luckily (or so I thought at the time), I had no endorsements, so I was free to create my own ensembles for matches.

A few weeks before the French Open I looked in the tennis shops around my home and picked outfits that weren't necessarily tennis skirts and shirts. There was a green skirt with polka dots and a Lycra roll of pink and purple at the waist; another skirt had ruffles . . . But going to a tournament like that meant a lot more than picking out clothing.

The French Open at Roland Garros Stadium and Wimbledon were the only Grand Slam tournaments I used to watch on television back home. They were the stadiums I knew as a child, and the ones I fantasized about. The day I arrived in Paris I went to see the stadium. It was empty, and I climbed high into the stands and sat down; I must have been there for at least an hour, getting the feel of the place, wondering what it would be like to play there, hoping that I'd make it to the quarters or semifinals. I remember it was quiet, almost reverent there. Usually there's so much noise and activity in an arena, but for that hour there was no buzz, no excitement, just peace. "Maybe one day I'll win this tournament," I whispered into the silence.

The first two rounds went pretty easily. Then came the third, against Zina Garrison. I have nothing to lose, I told myself in the locker room before the match. I'm playing the French Open against a top ten player, and I'm just going to do my best and enjoy being out in this stadium.

"Let's go, guys, it's time for the match," one of the tournament directors called. I took a deep breath and walked down the corridor that led to center court. As I walked, two little girls who were friends of my parents handed me a bouquet of red roses. I entered the stadium with my arms full of roses, my ears ringing with the cheers of the spectators, and my heart pounding in anticipation. I turned and tossed the roses to some fans — I couldn't really keep them on court with me, and thought the gesture would be nice.

It was a tight match. Zina is a volley player who has her best results on supreme court and grass. On clay she tends to play back, but always does well. Red clay is one of my favorite surfaces, and I played some great tennis. I won the match in two sets, 6–3, 6–2.

At the post-match press conference, I was ready to be noticed. I'd played well, was set to play against Jo-Anne Faull and, if I won that game, Manuela Maleeva in the quarterfinals, and was prepared to talk about the matches played and to come. "Monica, why'd you throw the roses?" a reporter called out. "What were you symbolizing," another yelled. "Why red roses?" a third chimed in. "Why not white or yellow?"

What is this? I thought in wonder. What are they asking me about?

It seemed that throwing some roses to my fans made a bigger impact than I'd expected. That wasn't my objective. I had just tossed some flowers into the stands to be nice to the fans — and to get rid of them. The press conference was a wake-up call. For the first time I realized that, as I became more successful, everything I did would be scrutinized.

Come on, guys, I thought during the conference. If I get through the next round I will play Maleeva in the quarters. If I win, I might get to play Steffi Graf in the semifinals — the undisputed number one woman for two years! I'm a fifteen-year-old nobody who might get to play the greatest female player in the world — a woman who closes each match in forty minutes, and who intimidates everyone on the tour. But no, they just wanted to talk about the roses. They didn't even notice that I'd gone blonde, since I'd been of little interest before I played well at the French Open.

This is crazy, I thought after the conference. But there was no time to worry about the press and what they believed. I won the match against Jo-Anne Faull in two sets and prepared myself for the quarter-finals. Manuela Maleeva was the number six player in the world. She'd won the Italian Open in 1984, and the Olympic bronze in 1988.

Play your game, just play your game, I told myself as I stepped onto the court and we began the first set. And I did, and took the match from Maleeva in two sets, 6–3, 7–5. I'm going to play in the semifinals of a Grand Slam tournament, I thought in wonder. I'm going to play Steffi Graf in the French Open.

"Do the best you can do, Monica," my father said with a smile before the semis. I nodded and gave a little laugh — I was too nervous to talk. I was about to play Steffi, who was the fastest and strongest all-round player on tour.

I lost the first set, 6–3. This is great, I thought to myself. I didn't lose 6–1 or 6–0; things are going pretty good! And then I started playing better than good. I started playing very well. The second set ended, and this time I'd won it, 6–3.

I can't tell you why I won that second set, apart from the fact that my overall game was good. People have this idea that a player wins because of one thing — like a powerful serve, or great volleys. But to win a set one player just has to be hitting better than the other — all round. During that second set of the French Open I was better than Steffi Graf.

"Oh my God, I can maybe beat Steffi!" I thought in shock before the third set. I could tell that everyone in the stadium was surprised that Steffi hadn't defeated me in under an hour. That was a new experience for me — shocking the spectators, feeling the excitement of the crowd swell. There was so much electricity in the arena that I felt the hairs on my neck standing up. We began to play and fought until we were tied, 3 games apiece. I'm in this, I told myself with growing excitement. And then . . . *ping!*

I broke quite a few racket strings during that match against Steffi, once at the very moment I had the chance to break her serve. When a player breaks a string, she has to get a new racket. I find that I'm a little off for the next few points: the strings and handle are new, and they always feel a bit strange. When I switched rackets in the semis, I lost my momentum. I never fully recovered, and lost the third set, 6–3. Regardless of my racket strings, Steffi had outplayed me and won the match.

I wasn't disappointed with myself. At that point in my career I had nothing to prove, no prior wins to defend. It was more important that I'd learned three things at the 1989 French Open. First, that my spontaneous gestures would be scrutinized by the press, and that scrutiny would increase with each success. Second, that it was time to switch from gut strings to Technifiber synthetic ones. And third and most importantly, that I could play against opponents like Steffi. I hadn't won this time, but in my heart I believed that some day I would.

It wasn't going to happen at my first Wimbledon.

There are only two weeks between the French Open and the start of

Wimbledon — two weeks to train, and to adjust from red clay to grass. Wimbledon is magical and elusive. Part of it's the beautiful surroundings, the tea and strawberries, the royalty. But it's also that Wimbledon is the only tournament played on grass. And there's no way to really prepare, because the surface differs from day to day. Grass is a fast surface, but it changes with the weather. Rain makes it slippery, sun dries it out — the court can change drastically in the course of a day, or a match.

My father and I immediately began to practice. One afternoon Pete Sampras was working out on the court next to ours. "Look at him, Monica. You're seeing someone who will one day be the number one player in the world," my father prophesied.

"No way, Dad," I replied.

"What luck at my first Wimbledon," I grumbled as I walked onto court number two and prepared to play my first-round match. "I'm playing on grass, which I've never played on before, and I draw the biggest server in tennis for the first round!" My opponent's name was Brenda Schultz, and everyone on the tour feared her. Brenda stood over six feet tall and her serves sped across the net at 125 mph. I don't want to go out in the first round, I thought in frustration.

I won the first set, 7–6. I was thrilled, because there was just no way to return Brenda's serve when she hit a winner. Miss, miss, miss, I chanted in my head before each of her serves. In the first set she did. In the second, she didn't. I'd be up 40–love and Brenda would serve three aces and win the game. She took me, 6–1, for the second set.

I'm in trouble, I thought at the start of the third. I can't win if her serve stays right on. And it did until 4 all, when my prayers were answered. Brenda missed a key serve, and I was up, 5–4. Monica, you've got to hold your serve, I told myself. You've been out here for two and a half hours — don't let it go to 5–5. Finish it. And I did, and won the set, 6–4. I was exhausted, thrilled, and looking forward to my next match.

When you first start playing professional tennis there are certain milestones. Getting to the semifinals in the French Open was one. And when I made it to the last sixteen — the final sixteen women players at Wimbledon — that was another. I was on a roll, I thought. I was playing great tennis, I told myself. And then? Then I played Steffi Graf.

Center court, grass surface, Graf. It couldn't have been any better. That's what I thought when I walked onto the court. Princess Diana was watching the match — I could see her in the stands, and kept looking over at her throughout my match . . . which wasn't very long: it was over in what felt like fifteen minutes. I went onto the court, saw the Princess, hit a few balls, and left. Steffi beat me, 6–0, 6–1. Whatever I hit, she hit back a winner. She ran down everything — I didn't have a chance. I couldn't even be upset about the match. It had been too short to agonize over. And there was a silver lining. I had seen the Princess, and she'd seen me.

My next major tournament was the US Open in August 1989. It was my first time, and it would be Chris Evert's last. She had decided to retire that year. For that reason, when I looked at the draw for the tournament I was worried.

When I read the draw before a match, I always figure out who I'll play if I win. If I won my third-round match, I'd face Chris. And, while I wanted another chance to play her, I was torn. I didn't want to lose, because this was my first US Open and I wanted to try to reach the quarters or semis. But I also worried that if I won I'd be remembered as the girl who ended Chris's chance to finish her career with a US Open win. I was just a kid, and that really bothered me. Still, I won my third round.

I was weak-kneed as Chris and I stepped onto center court to play. The stands were packed, and the anticipation of the crowd was almost dizzying. Years later, Chris told me that she'd been really tense that day, too. She'd lost to me the last time we'd played, and she said she didn't want to end her career by losing to a fifteen-year-old kid. I never would have guessed it. She seemed poised and reserved. There was no way to tell she was nervous.

By contrast, I was rattled. The crowds, the noise, the excitement of playing on center court, were overwhelming. Chris Evert had the experience to tune all of those things out and play her game. She's a very steady back-court player, hardly ever misses her backhand, and hits close to the lines. That day Chris beat me, 6–0, 6–2. Someday, I thought as I walked off the court, I'll learn how to tune everything out but the game.

I was sad to lose, but also relieved. Chris lost in the next round to Zina Garrison, but she would always be a legend; no one could take that away from her.

That year, 1989, I played all my heroines: Steffi Graf, Chris Evert, and finally, and for the first time, Martina Navratilova. After the US Open, I went to Dallas, Texas, for a Virginia Slims tournament.

I almost missed my opportunity to play Martina. In the first round of the tournament I played a match against Bettina Bunge. I was up 5–1 in the first set and let Bettina come back to 5 all. It was the first time in my career that an opponent had staged such a comeback. It happens. Players who are down by a big margin lose their inhibitions. Sometimes that allows them to play brilliant tennis. I told myself right then that I'd never let anybody do that to me again. It was too nerve-racking. I learned a valuable lesson that round: the set is never closed, the match is never over, until you shake hands at the net. Most importantly, I won the match and the chance to play Martina in the finals.

Supreme courts are blue, fast, and, after grass, Martina Navratilova's favorite surface. But I didn't think about that as I stepped out to play my childhood hero. And I didn't think about what a powerful player Martina was, or how she ran down everything. Instead, I focused on enjoying the moment. The first set was a battle which I lost. The second I won, and in the third Martina closed me down. It was a good match, a tough one, and I was proud of my game. Most importantly, that match earned me the right to play with the best in tennis.

I had qualified for the 1989 Virginia Slims Championships in November. At the end of each tennis season Virginia Slims held a tournament at Madison Square Garden in New York City for the top sixteen women players in the world. After one season as a professional, I had earned my place as one of those women.

I lost to Martina in an early round of the championships, but not without a fight. I was down 4–1 and I came back and won that set. And I think that's when I began to have a reputation as a tenacious player. The media started writing that I was mentally strong, and that great things were expected of me in 1990. It was strange to read, and not to feel pressure. It had been an unbelievable year for me: my first as a professional, and I was already ranked sixth in the world. The media began saying that next year I'd be in the top three. I tried not to read the papers after I'd read that.

My goal as a tennis player, even at fifteen, was to go out on the court and play well; not win a match, just play well. Now that I was expected to be in the top three, the focus seemed to shift toward winning, and I didn't want that. I've never wanted that.

$$\left(12 \right)$$

I was already letting them down. That's all I could think after I was eliminated by Ros Fairbank in the first round of the February 1990 Virginia Slims tournament in Chicago. The press had expected so much from me after my '89 season. Maybe they'd been wrong, I thought as I packed my duffle and left the stadium. I went back to the hotel and iced my shoulder, which had begun to hurt pretty badly. I'd played so many matches in 1989 that my joint and rotator cuff were inflamed from over-use. I felt disheartened, but decided to take a few weeks off to heal, and then fight to win my next match.

It didn't happen. I went to the Virginia Slims of Boca Raton. There was a lot of media attention for the tournament because a young phenom named Jennifer Capriati was going to play her first professional match. Jennifer was thirteen at the time, and already had millions in endorsements before she stepped out onto the court. The press hoped that we would play each other in the finals — two young, aggressive players battling it out. But like I said, it didn't happen.

"What's wrong with me?" I asked myself in frustration after I lost my third-round match. I went to the locker room and slumped into a chair. "Why am I playing so badly?" An overwhelming sense of disappointment and frustration settled over me.

"Monica . . . can I give you some advice?" Leslie Allen, a former player and a staff member of the WTA, asked me in the locker room. I nodded. "Some days are bad, that's just the way it goes. You've just got to stick with it . . . and try not to be so hard on yourself."

It was the first time that anyone with the tour had taken the time to say a kind word, offer some advice. It meant a lot to me. I was a professional whose life revolved around tennis, but I was also a sixteen-year-old. There are so many emotions and issues that a teenager has to deal with — friends, school, boys, insecurities. I was no different. Since I spent most of my time on the court, those issues came out in the locker room, during practice and, like it or not, during matches.

Jennifer made it to the finals and then lost in a good match against Gabriela Sabatini. It was a great accomplishment for her first professional tournament, and it took the focus and some of the pressure off me at a time when I needed space. The media was enamored with Jennifer. She was now the youngest rising star, which meant that for a while I didn't have to live up to their expectations.

I focused on healing my shoulder, which was still giving me problems, and on practicing with my father at the academy. We didn't really change anything; I just tried to forget about rankings, winning, and what other people assumed I might do in 1990. And it worked.

In mid-March I went to play the Lipton Championship in Key Biscayne, Florida. Lipton is the fifth biggest tournament in the world. One match at a time, I told myself when I got to the tournament. Don't look at the draw, Monica, just focus on who you're playing at the moment. And I did . . . until the fourth round.

Ros Fairbank. Ros, who'd beaten me in the first round of the Virginia Slims of Chicago, was my fourth-round opponent at Lipton. "Great, just when I thought I was on the upswing, I've got to play her again." When I'm nervous, I talk to myself. Sitting in the locker room before the match, I gave myself a lecture. "Give it a chance, Monica," I said. "You've had a few weeks of rest, you're playing good tennis. Just play your game and maybe the outcome will be better."

I need to win this match for my sake, I thought as I stepped onto the court. I need this one. Ros is a serve-and-volley player, and passing shots were an important part of beating her. That day I never lost control. I felt strong, unafraid, and played the game that I play in practice. I took Ros, 6–3, 6–4, in fairly easy sets.

Whew, I was relieved! Beating Ros was just the shot of confidence I needed before playing my next match. I'd peeked at the draw and knew I would face Jennifer Capriati if she won her fourth-round match. It would have been our first encounter, but in the end it didn't happen at Lipton.

Jennifer was upset by a French player and I beat Nathalie Tauziat in the semifinals, 6–3, 6–1, and Judith Wiesner, 6–1, 6–2, in an easy finals match. I had won Lipton! It was great to turn around my season. I'd done so poorly for the last three months, and I had really needed a big win to rebuild my confidence. My father and I went to San Antonio for another tournament. Once again, I won. We hopped on a plane back to Florida after the match. Both of us were excited by my game, and ready to focus on the next big match of the spring, the Italian Open.

"What court can I take?" I asked the organizational director at the academy the morning after I returned. The man didn't answer me. "Is there a basket of balls out here I can use?"

"We have no court for you," he finally replied.

"Well, okay," I said. I was disappointed, because I needed a morning practice. "What time should I come back for a court?"

"You can't get a court later, either," the coach explained.

"Why?" my father interjected. At that point we were both confused, puzzled.

"The coaches at the academy have been instructed that you can no longer have courts here," he told us.

"*What?!*" my father and I said in unison. We tried to get to the bottom of the problem, but it was no use. No one would give us a straight answer. There was nothing for us to do, so we left the academy courts and went to look for a public court to practice on.

Nick Bollettieri's way of sorting things out is through letters — always has been. A few days later we received a letter from Nick which said in effect: "Sorry our relationship ended this way, but I saw no reason for going forward . . ."

No reason for going forward? To this day, I'm not certain why Nick kicked me out of the academy. Nick's treatment of me wasn't an anomaly. There are many tennis players who have had similar experiences with him. Even Andre's relationship with Nick ended with letters. Still, I truly believe Nick is a great human being in his heart. He gave scholarships to so many kids who loved tennis.

My situation with Nick was more complicated than I understood at fourteen, fifteen, sixteen years of age. Nick didn't handle our relationship the way I would have hoped, but I will always be grateful for my academy scholarship — and to Nick's associate, Dr. Apu Kutton, for his kindness.

There was no time to dwell on the situation. I had a month before the Italian Open, and no courts to practice on. We had been living in a condominium in Bradenton, close to the academy. Now we had to find a new place to live that had private tennis courts. For the week before my next tournament I practiced on public courts in Sarasota. The courts were usually full, so I had to wait for a court and then pay by the hour. They were hard courts, and my next tournament was the Eckerd Open on clay. I won anyway. It was my third win in a row. For the first time I was on a winning streak.

"This isn't working, Monica," my father said ruefully as we waited for court time after our return from Tampa. A few days later my parents found a small house in a community in Sarasota. There were private courts there, and Dad and I were so pleased to get back to our regular training schedule. But it didn't happen. The people who lived in our new neighborhood loved their tennis so much that I couldn't get on a court until the afternoons. Once again we took what we could get, and began to focus on the Italian Open.

Until that May of 1990 I never believed I could beat Steffi, Chris, Gaby or Martina unless I got incredibly lucky — I'd put those players on such a high pedestal. The Italian Open was a turning point in my career. I went to Italy full of anticipation and excitement, hoping to get to the finals, hoping for a chance to play one of the top five women in the world. Steffi wasn't playing, but Martina was there, and I wanted the chance to face her again. I got my wish by defeating Maleeva in the quarters and Kelesi in the semifinals.

Playing Martina is always tough. She can mix it up really well, and she's a left hander like me. It's difficult for a left hander to return another lefty's serve because it comes at such a severe angle. It's also strange to play a lefty (most players are right handed) because everything is opposite and it takes a while to get used to the switch. By the time I feel comfortable, the match is usually over.

The finals of the Italian Open was the quickest match I'd ever played. It felt like 1989 when Steffi dismissed me off the grass at Wimbledon, except this time I was in control. Every shot was a winner and I had no inhibitions, held nothing back. I won the Italian Open, 6–1, 6–1 — I'd beaten Martina.

At the post-match press conference Martina told the media she "felt like she'd been run over by a truck." As I sat facing the cameras and microphones I finally realized that maybe I was better than I thought. I remembered the set I'd taken off Martina at the '89 championships at Madison Garden. I had been so certain I'd just been lucky. Maybe, I marveled, it wasn't luck.

Perhaps it was a blessing that in 1990 I didn't understand the baggage attached to my growing success. Tennis was still a game of numbers to me, of serves, volleys, overheads and winners. If I'd known that Günther Parche was starting to follow my career, allowing his dark thoughts to overwhelm his senses until I became his obsession, his target, I'm not sure how it would've affected my game. As it was, I had until April 1993 before I finally understood that tennis wasn't just a game of love, but of life and death.

(13)

To: Office of Public Prosecutions at the Regional Court of Hamburg

Subject: Mr. Günther Parche, born on July 4, 1954, in Herigen, Germany

PSYCHIATRIC EXPERT'S OPINION ON MR. PARCHE, IN WHICH THE ISSUE OF CRIMINAL RESPONSIBILITY IS TO BE ASSESSED

After a brief introductory conversation and after the suspect had been advised of his rights, it quickly became apparent to both interrogating officers that he had mental defects. He had a very simple vocabulary and all his thoughts revolved around Steffi Graf. We were given the impression that she was the most important person to him. He idolizes her. The suspect repeatedly declared that he would do anything for her . . .

"Ms. Pickart, Mr. Parche's aunt, stated the following for the record . . . Parche was a quiet boy. He had been unemployed since 1991 . . . In response to a question about his mental state, Ms. Pickart stated that he was completely normal. According to Ms. Pickart's statement, he took every defeat suffered by Miss Graf hard, so that he became taciturn and even displayed outbursts of rage . . .

"In response to a question, Mr. Parche said that he had had no traumatic experiences during his childhood. He had never suffered from anxiety, but was unable to say whether there was a prolonged period of bedwetting or whether he chewed his fingernails . . .

"He spent most of his leisure time at home; he rarely went into the village or visited a pub; he was not a member of any club . . . he had had no contact with the female sex in recent years because he was shy. Sexuality was a subject about which he barely spoke, as it was embarrassing for him and he either evaded questions on this subject or did not answer them . . .

"Mr. Parche decided to leave his hometown in May of 1990 and travel to West Germany ('that had to do with Stephanie Graf'). In May of 1990 she lost a tournament against Seles in Berlin, which the people in the village and his co-workers at the factory talked and teased him about, as he had revealed that he was a fan of Graf's. He had been tormented by Steffi Graf's defeat and the reaction of his neighbors, and had thought of suicide ('I did not know how though') . . .

"Partly to avoid the ridicule of his colleagues and partly because of the overall economic situation, he left his job after his return . . . In the following years he was unemployed, so he worked at home, in the yard and garden, living off his aunt and his savings . . .

"He was interested in sports, although he had never participated in any; he watched sport on television, and soccer was a favorite . . . This changed after Stephanie Graf had become established as one of the best international female tennis players. While he was unaffected by Boris Becker's successes, he watched Stephanie Graf's games with increasing adulation, and by 1985/86, he was an enthusiastic Graf fan. He read in depth about the rules of the game, knew what a volley or a slice was, researched Stephanie Graf's biography, but also knew quite a bit about her opponents . . .

"The investigation disclosed that he was interested in Graf primarily as a person, not in the type of sport [she played]; he would have been interested in her even if she had been a track and field athlete or a fencer . . .

"With shining eyes, he described 'her fantastic figure,' her 'radiant eyes,' and pointed out that she 'had the nicest legs of all the female players.' He continued enthusiastically: 'Stephanie Graf is a dream, not only as an athlete, but also as a human being, she is a role model for us all, has a big heart.'. . .

"Even though he had lived very modestly in the former GDR and had saved quite a bit, in 1988 he decided to spend DM 10,000 in East German money on a video recorder just to be able to record her games and watch them once again later on ('I would have spent DM20,000, just to see her once more, I would not have spent even DM1,000 for any other player.') . . .

"Parche had already attempted to obtain magazines in the former GDR in order to look at photos of Stephanie Graf. He then photographed these magazine pictures, enlarged them, and hung them up in his room. He also repeatedly wrote to her, sent her flowers and even money for her birthdays, but did not feel confident enough to give his name as the sender . . . In his letters he advised her not to take any risks and asked her to be careful when driving, in order not to have an accident . . .

"Over the years he idealized Stephanie Graf more and more ('she is almost as important to me as God'); he thought she was as important as the Pope or the President of the United States of America . . . He . . . never tried to make direct contact with Stephanie Graf and could not imagine meeting her. He felt that he would freeze up if he actually met her; his heart would stand still . . .

"Parche . . . occupied himself with Stephanie Graf practically every day and of course watched every tournament of hers. Days before the final or the semifinals, he would be very excited, could hardly eat anything, slept poorly, and had a sensation of heaviness at the pit of his stomach. If the game went smoothly and without any problems; if she won, then he was the happiest man and sometimes cried for ten minutes . . . If she lost, he went into a depression which lasted for days, and he even occasionally developed suicidal intentions during important tournaments . . .

"When Seles won over Graf in the final game at Berlin in 1990, he was 'shattered.' When Seles ('she is not pretty, women shouldn't be as thin as a bone') went on to establish herself as the number one in the tennis world, he was under permanent pressure. He constantly desired and even prayed that she would break an arm or leg or suffer another injury so that she would be out of the game for a while . . .

"After Monica Seles had become the number one in women's tennis, Mr. Parche had thought of actively doing something for Stephanie Graf . . . He wanted to 'teach Monica Seles a lesson' . . .

"He decided to stab [Seles] in the game against Maleeva . . . He did not want to stab her in the head, but he was unable to reach her arm, so he aimed for the back . . .

"During the course of his pre-trial detention, he had also had thoughts of suicide but had not dared to take this step ('somebody might have thought that Stephanie Graf had bribed me to do the attack') . . .

EVALUATION

". . . On the basis of the detailed examinations conducted and the observations made, it is assumed by this expert that a development had commenced in Mr. Parche with respect to the relationship with Stephanie Graf which had not assumed any psychotic traits . . . yet was clearly pathologically depraved. It reflected an unreal idealization, probably unconscious sexual elements and a fanaticism, which went as far as self-sacrifice. When taking his basic character structure into consideration, it is this expert's opinion that this personality disorder corresponds to a severe mental abnormality of the type that massively affected his control mechanisms at the time of the crime, so that a considerable reduction of his ability to control himself cannot be ruled out, at least."

As May 1993 progressed, I grew more distant. I started to take long drives through the mountains — no direction, no destination. Sometimes my mother would come with me; sometimes I'd leave our hotel in Vail and return many hours later. It felt so safe in the car — doors locked, silence everywhere. Best of all, no one knew where I was going . . . not even me.

By June I was driving for hours on end. The press had left me alone for the most part, but there were still a few reporters in Vail waiting to get an exclusive. They couldn't talk to me because they couldn't find me.

Things weren't all bad. During those months in Vail I received a lot of nice mail from fans. In addition, Michael J. Fox, Barbara Walters, Michael Bolton and a lot of other celebrities sent flowers. Their support meant a lot.

None of the top players sent letters or flowers, which really hurt my feelings. Steffi didn't call to see how I was until December. She told the press that she'd tried to call me after the attack, but she couldn't get my number. Steffi knew I was represented by IMG: all she had to do was call the offices and my manager would have put us in touch. Meanwhile, the tour went on without me and I felt lost.

The tennis court had been my domain. There, I was invincible and untouchable. When Parche stabbed me, he took all that away and showed me that I couldn't believe all the people who said I'd be safe, no matter what.

I was stabbed in the back. That was the bottom line. I couldn't stop repeating it in my head. It was difficult to maintain Dr. Steadman's physical therapy regimen: I'd try to go to the gym for light exercise, try to eat well and get a lot of sleep, but I just couldn't seem to do it. I'd break into tears at odd moments and I found it hard to get out of bed in the morning.

Dr. Steadman and Dr. Hawkins tried to help me. They said that my behavior wasn't typical, although they'd never dealt with an athlete who'd been stabbed. Still, athletes usually stick to their training, because they're desperate to get back to their sport. Dr. Steadman has done a lot of work with the US ski team; he suggested that I go and see their clinical psychologist, Dr. Jerry May. "He might be able to help you work through your emotions," he said.

"I'm still physically recovering," I replied. "Maybe when my shoulder feels a bit better . . ."

I procrastinated for almost a month. I was afraid to spend time with a stranger — I didn't trust anyone new. But I was still crying every day, still having irrational thoughts and nightmares.

By July I was so desperate I took a flight to Lake Tahoe, California, to see Dr. May for ten days. I'd never been to a psychologist: walking into his office, I didn't know what to expect. I'm a strong person; he's not going to make me cry, I thought as I sat down.

On that first meeting, I failed to open up to Dr. May: I didn't let on that I had a problem. I just described my physical therapy, and said that there were moments when I didn't feel very positive, but that I could control them. I don't know whether or not Dr. May believed me. At the end of the session all he said was, "Monica, I think it's really important for you to continue your therapy. As the months since the attack pass, you might have a harder time dealing with it than you think. You might need some help working through this, and I'm here if you need me."

Over the next week we began to discuss the attack in a general way. I told Dr. May that I wished I'd never gone to Hamburg; that I wished the attack hadn't happened; that I wanted to be at Wimbledon at that moment, not sitting in his office. I never admitted that I relived the attack every night — I didn't feel comfortable discussing those things with a man I'd just met. I did, however, spend a lot of time crying. Once I started, I just couldn't stop. We often had to end our session because Dr. May couldn't make any sense of what I was saying. I just couldn't put together the sentence: "Günther Parche stabbed me and I have nightmares about the knife." I couldn't say that I was unable to imagine myself walking out on a tennis court again, sitting with my back to the spectators; that I was afraid my career was over. The words just wouldn't come out.

When I left Lake Tahoe, I told Dr. May I'd call to schedule another ten-day session. Looking back now, I realize that I wasn't ready to face my memories. I'd have to spend more time trying to outrun, out-exercise and out-eat my demons before I was ready to ask him for help.

But there was *one* thing I was ready to do. In August of 1993 I agreed to hold one definitive interview to stop all the speculation and rumors about how I was faring since the attack. Originally, I didn't want to do an interview because I felt I had nothing to say. However, I'd received calls from Barbara Walters, Connie Chung, Jane Pauley, Charles Gibson, Bryant Gumbel, Katie Couric and all the other top television interviewers, and it was clear to me that it was time to answer their questions.

I believe that any of the celebrity journalists who contacted me would have done a great job, but I chose Diane Sawyer to interview me after watching her recent interview on anorexia.

The interview was taped at a resort near my home in Florida, in a mini television studio ABC built in a room overlooking the ocean. I was nervous on the day of the interview, but determined to answer Diane's questions openly and honestly. I wanted to move away from the stabbing, and I believed the interview was an important step.

The questions came tough and fast: What was it like to be stabbed? When are you returning? How do you feel about the other players voting not to hold your ranking? How are your parents coping? What are you doing with your time? Are you practicing? How are you physically?

How are you emotionally? Have you watched the tape of the stabbing? How do you feel when you watch tournaments in which you know you should be playing?

The interview was new territory for everyone. No top athlete had ever been stabbed in the middle of a sporting event, and ABC was as sensitive about the questions as possible. Still, up until the interview I'd been surrounded by friends and family who didn't ask the kinds of questions that Diane did. It was a hard day.

I broke down several times during the taping, but insisted on continuing with the interview. Diane was kind and patient, and during breaks we spent some private time walking along the beach and the grounds of the resort. A few days later the interview came onto the air. The public reaction was positive, and the rumors about me did stop — for about a month . . .

There are many ways to escape depression. One of them is to keep moving. After my ten-day session with Dr. May and my interview with Diane Sawyer, my mother and I flew to Los Angeles. From there, we planned to return to Vail so that I could rehab and get on a training regimen. Our flight back to Vail left the next morning, so we went to a hotel room for the night. As I walked into the elevator, I looked up to see Betsy Nagelsen standing across from me. Both our jaws dropped.

Betsy knew me before I knew her. The first time she saw me play I was just thirteen years old. Nick Bollettieri had brought some of his phenoms over to Orlando, Florida, for an exhibition at a gated community called Isleworth. For the exhibition Zoltan hit balls to me on the run, and I returned them to a square box made of tennis balls in the corners of his court. I rarely missed my shots, even though Zoltan was hitting at me really hard.

Betsy and her friend, Susie Mascarin, both professional players on the tour, were sitting in the stands. Betsy told me years later that Susie had watched me hitting ball after ball, every one hard and accurate. After fifteen minutes she leaned over to Betsy and said, "Yeah, it's time to have kids." She did, and she's happily married and raising a family.

I've talked to Betsy about that day. Did she know then that I was going to be a great player? I asked her. Betsy says that it was clear I had "it." Whether "it" is killer instinct, talent, intense concentration, total desire, or a refusal to lose, she didn't know. But she says she could see the gift, just as she could tell that I was a polite and very concerned person. "A serving type of person," is how she put it.

....

Maybe that's why Betsy called me in 1991 and asked me to be her doubles partner for a Slims tournament. Though I didn't normally play doubles matches, I said yes. I had already partnered her in 1990, I had no friends on the tour, and was drawn to Betsy. She was more full of life than anyone I know — bursting with energy and enthusiasm. I wanted to be a part of that.

We began to play more doubles together. During the following two years we had a fun relationship — shopping, pancake-eating, lightness and laughter. I always looked forward to playing with Betsy, and to the good times we'd have after the match. It was the first friendship I'd ever had on the tour — the only true friendship I've ever had with a professional tennis player. It was possible for several reasons. First, Betsy had already had an impressive career — she was the number one junior player in the world and had wins against greats like Chris Evert. When our friendship began, Betsy wasn't a top ten singles player. That meant we weren't competing with each other. Second, Betsy was older than me, and we were at different points in our careers.

After the attack Betsy and her husband, Mark McCormack, kept in touch with Stephanie Tolleson to see how I was recuperating. Betsy didn't want to call me directly, because she wanted to allow me my privacy. Still, she wanted me to know that she and Mark were thinking of me. In June she called me directly. I think she sensed that my world had been blown off its axis and that I had no idea how to get back on track. Betsy made it clear that she was there for me if I needed her. I didn't know then that she'd be one of the key people in my recovery.

I didn't see Betsy until July 1993 in that hotel elevator in Los Angeles. I was so startled that I barely said two words during the ride to our floor. Betsy returned to her room, but minutes later she called me. "Mark and I are going to Palm Desert," Betsy said. "I've got a great idea. Why don't you and your mom come with us?"

Why not? Mom and I followed Betsy and Mark to Palm Desert in our rental car. When we got to the condominium, I didn't really feel like doing anything. Betsy can't stand doing nothing, so she suggested we rent a convertible and she'd teach me how to drive a stick-shift. It was 125 degrees in Palm Desert, but Betsy is pretty convincing. An hour later I was behind the wheel of a fire-engine-red Miata.

"Rip it out, take it to the floor." Betsy laughed as I gingerly tried to shift from second to third. "It's a rental, Monica," she reminded me in exasperation, "go for it!"

I'm such a cautious person that I wanted to learn slowly, but Betsy's enthusiasm was catching. It took all day, but I finally got the hang of stick-shift. It was the most fun I'd had in months.

"Let's get Mark and your mom and show them what you can do," Betsy suggested. We loaded them in to the car, and took off. There was a lot of laughter that day — it felt strange, but good.

During our stay in Palm Desert Betsy got the chance to see first hand how I was handling the attack. There were moments, like in the car, that I felt my depression begin to lift. And there were other times when not even Betsy could coax me out of my room. After that week she made a concerted effort to get me to come to her home in Orlando, or out skiing in Vail. Visiting her always gave me a much needed respite from my depression. Over the next two years our friendship would develop into a close bond.

Mom and I were both sad to leave Palm Desert, but it was time to return to Vail and my physical therapy. I felt depression settle like gravity on my shoulders as our plane headed down the runway.

Once again, my rehabilitation didn't go as well as the doctors had hoped. I couldn't stay on track. I'd do my physical therapy, but couldn't seem to get on the treadmill to begin my cardiovascular training. Instead, I'd hop in the car and try to outrun the bad feelings that were beginning to cling to my mind like dead leaves, crunching everywhere I went. I'd wander through the woods and then sit cross-legged in the middle of nowhere, allowing my mind to focus on childhood memories, Parche, and the knife that stabbed into me. Late July and early August passed in an all-too-familiar haze.

It was Arthur Ashe who momentarily brought me back to reality. In

1991 I had pulled out of Wimbledon because of an injury, but had failed to explain my actions to the press. The result was months of rumors, and an intense media barrage. During a difficult time, Arthur gave me support. In 1993 I had the opportunity to return the favor.

The first Arthur Ashe Day exhibition in support of AIDS was held in August of 1992, just before the US Open. I was proud to attend that benefit. Arthur died on February 6, 1993 from the disease and the 1993 Arthur Ashe Day would be the first without its benefactor. I couldn't miss the opportunity to pay tribute to such a great man. I wanted to support his family and remind them how much Arthur was still loved.

I was extremely worried about my decision to travel to New York. It would be my first public appearance in four months. I'd been avoiding the press, not to antagonize them but because I had nothing to say. I could barely accept the fact that I'd been stabbed, much less talk about my plans to return to the game. At that point I was still having difficulty raising my arm, and I had yet to hit a tennis ball.

Over the next few months my silence would begin to frustrate the media and, in an effort to get me to talk, some reporters would release stories claiming that I'd committed myself to playing various tournaments in the near future. My manager, Stephanie Tolleson, tried to stop those reports, and to explain that I had no immediate plans to return to the game. But the damage was already done.

We didn't alert the press about my decision to attend Arthur Ashe Day. It was the only way we could be certain that security would be air-tight when I arrived in New York. I didn't feel comfortable appearing in public, and keeping my plans secret made me feel better.

It was hard to walk into the Flushing Meadows stadium, knowing that I couldn't play in the Open that year. It tore at my heart not to be part of the tournament; it tore at my mind to know why. As I went up to sit with Jeanne Ashe and her daughter, Camera, the spectators recognized me. They stood up and began to cheer and clap. I started laughing and crying. For a change, they were tears of happiness and appreciation.

As the players filed out onto the court for the tournament, some waved to me and I waved back. Aranxta Sanchez Vicario was the only female player who actually came up to my box and sat down to talk. I really appreciated her kindness. Wimbledon winner Michael Stich also spoke to me, and the support of Mayor Dinkins, who was a tennis fan and a friend and who kept in touch throughout my recovery, meant a great deal. However, none of the other top players came over to me.

"Monica, they want you to have a press conference," Bob Kain (the head of racket sports at IMG) told me that afternoon.

"I'm just here to support the Ashe family," I replied.

"I think you should do it," Bob said. "We've had thousands of requests for interviews, and this is a good opportunity to give the media what they want. If you don't, they're going to say you think you're too big to hold a press conference."

"And if I do, they're going to say I'm trying to steal the headlines," I said.

It was a lose-lose situation, we both agreed, but Bob still thought I should do the conference.

I held a press conference on Monday, the first day of the US Open. I didn't want to step on anyone's toes. I knew that all the top players would win their matches fairly easily, so it would be the best day to hold the conference. I was nervous, but it went very well until the last question.

"Monica, has Steffi tried to contact you since the attack? Have you talked to her since the hospital visit in Hamburg?"

I didn't know what to say. There was no easy way out without telling a lie. I didn't want to lie, so I told the truth. "No, I haven't heard from Steffi since Hamburg," I carefully replied. "We had an emotional visit in my hospital room, and Steffi said she'd call me. I wish she had, but she hasn't." The conference ended and I felt pretty good about how I'd handled all the questions.

The following morning there were two New York tabloids outside my hotel room door. The headlines on the first were in support of Seles, saying how terribly Steffi had acted after the attack. The second was in defense of Graf. It said that I had called her rude at the press conference, and that I blamed her for the stabbing because Parche had been one of her fans. I never, ever, said that. The tabloids took two little questions and turned them into a war between Steffi and me. They wanted us to hate each other because that sold papers.

I left New York confused. What had initially been a difficult trip, made solely to support the memory of Arthur Ashe, had turned into another unfortunate situation. I was tired of unfortunate situations. I just couldn't seem to win.

After the press conference I just wanted to go somewhere that would take my mind off the US Open. I didn't want to watch it, to imagine who I'd be playing . . . if I was playing. It was time to run again.

I'd always wanted to see a Formula One car race: something about the speed really attracts me to the sport. There's so much excitement at those races. The drivers don't just go round in circles; they navigate different shaped courses. I was always playing tennis during the Formula season, so I'd never had the opportunity to see a live race.

Mom and I flew to Italy for the races, where I got to meet Ayrton Senna, my favorite driver, and Mario Andretti, who was trying to make the switch from the 500 to Formula One. The drivers were great to talk to. They'd heard about the attack, and they discussed it with me sensitively. They told me about the dangers they faced on the track every time they drove, and how they handled their fears. Ayrton told me about his own philosophy on life — "You never know when it's going to end," he said, "so live every day."

It was great to be in Italy, to watch those cars zooming around the track, and to be completely detached from the US Open. I didn't realize then that I was establishing a pattern where I tried to keep distracted and busy in order to prevent myself from thinking about the attack. And it was only later, when I couldn't travel, couldn't work out until I fell into bed exhausted, that I finally had to face the issues and memories that had been on my tail for almost a year.

*   *   *

I flew back to Vail and stepped up my therapy to include swinging a tennis racket in the basement of Dr. Steadman and Dr. Hawkins's clinic. They'd understood that I was afraid to step back onto a court, so they'd created a makeshift one for me in their basement. I felt some pain in my shoulder each time I swung, but it was lessening. A few weeks later I flew back home to Florida: to my home, my family, and the empty tennis court in my backyard.

Meanwhile, lawyers in Germany prepared for Parche's impending trial. They gathered statements from witnesses, psychiatrists and family members. In the end, all those testimonies wouldn't make any difference. But as I returned home to sort through the broken shards of my life, I was certain of only one thing: Günther Parche would be found guilty and made to take responsibility for his crime.

16

STATE CRIMINAL INVESTIGATION DEPARTMENT (LKA) 211
1993

Re: Grievous Bodily Harming of Monica Seles

WITNESS TESTIMONY

*"I am a sports student and for two years have been employed in connection
with the ladies' tennis tournament for this week of tennis.*

*"For the match between Monica Seles and Magdalena Maleeva, my job
was to sit behind Monica Seles's bench and ensure that she did not hang her
coat over the advertisement carriers. I sat at about seat 34 or 35, that is,
diagonally to the left behind Monica Seles . . .*

*"Then, at some point I looked in Monica Seles's direction again. I could
see a man now standing behind her. I could see the man turning. In my
opinion he was holding a plastic or cloth bag in his hand. Then I saw him
raise both hands up high over his head and strike them forwards. It looked
to me as if he were going to hit her. At that point I had not yet seen a knife
in the man's hand. It looked to me as if he had struck once.*

*"As he raised his hands to hit her a second time he was already being
pulled back by the security guard. Together with other spectators, we then
overpowered the man. Whilst we were overpowering him I also saw the knife
in his right hand. His fist was clenched around the handle and the blade was
jutting out downwards . . .*

"In response to your question, I can say that Monica Seles leaned forward

slightly, probably to wipe her face with the towel, just at the moment the man 'hit' her. His 'hitting' her and her leaning forward happened practically parallel to each other."

CRIMINAL POLICE STATION WESTERSTEDE
May 26, 1993

WITNESS TESTIMONY

"On April 30, 1993, I went to Hamburg Rothenbaum and watched the tennis match with Monica Seles. I sat in the third row. It must have been ten to seven or so when Monica Seles came to the side of the court to get something. She sat on the bench and bent forwards. At that moment, I saw a man's right arm with a knife in the hand. The knife was approximately twenty cm long with the handle. The man stabbed Monica Seles in her back. However, he did not stab her very fast with the knife so that I had the impression that the man might be drunk. At that moment, he was already overwhelmed by another man and taken away. I can't describe the man himself in more detail. But I do know that it was the man with the knife who was then overwhelmed and taken away by the others. I can't say anything else about this matter."

WITNESS TESTIMONY

". . . On Friday, April 30, 1993 I watched the Ladies' tennis tournament at Rothenbaum in Hamburg together with a friend. I was sitting in the first row behind the bench where Monica Seles was sitting. The distance was one or two meters.

"At the end of a break, a man went past me; he wore an Arthur Ashe cap and carried a shopping bag and a jacket in his hands. It was clear that

he had come down from the stairs on the right-hand side. I noticed the man especially because he was quite clearly not a tennis fan. I noticed especially that he did not have a camera. When the man was directly behind Monica Seles, I saw that he raised both hands and moved them toward Monica Seles's back. Monica had bent forward, I think that she wanted to put something down. The referee had already called 'time.'

"In reply to a question, I state that I first did not see any weapon in the man's hand. He must have concealed the knife under the jacket or under the shopping bag. Immediately after attacking Monica, he was overwhelmed by one of her bodyguards. When this was happening, the knife fell out of his hand. It landed directly in front of my feet. The knife had a turquoise-colored handle, the blade was ten to fifteen cm long. I saw no blood on the knife . . . Later I also saw that Monica was bleeding from her back."

17

In early October 1993 I started hitting with my dad. It just happened — we didn't plan it. For weeks I just stared at the court. I'd walk to the edge, think about stepping onto the surface, and then turn around and go back inside. Finally, the inactivity got to me. I wasn't in Palm Desert, or Italy, or Vail. There weren't any race cars, stick-shift lessons, or mountains to distract me. I had to do something to quiet the voices in my head — the ones that said Parche was going to hurt me again; the ones that screamed in the night.

Dad stood on my side of the net and tossed balls to me. He threw them softly, underhand. I tried to hit them back, but my shots flew everywhere. I'd lost my touch. My serves were wild, out of control. At first, I only did small serves — I was afraid something was going to pop or pull in my shoulder. It felt strange to be on the court again, stranger still to have no control of the ball. Thoughts about the attack fell away as I concentrated. Stepping out onto the court had been the toughest part. After that, I felt oddly at peace. Physical exertion was clearly the answer.

In September I had begun to train with Bob Kersee, the husband and coach of the great Olympic champion Jackie Joyner-Kersee, because my dad thought it might be fun for me and take my mind off negative things. Every morning Bob and I ran several miles. Then we went to the gym and lifted weights, and in the afternoon I'd work with my dad. Some days Jackie would join us for our morning workout. I'd look over at her and think, That's what being an athlete is — her body was perfectly toned and muscled, and she was an all-round nice person.

"Stay positive, Monica," she would say when I'd had a tough day. "There's been a lot of days I didn't want to work hard, but in the end it'll pay off."

Every night I fell into bed aching with exhaustion. The dreams still came, but less frequently. I was too tired to dream. I trained with Bob and Jackie six days a week for ten weeks, from late September to the end of October and early November to just before Christmas. I watched my body change, become more defined. I was getting into the best shape of my life. Most important, I wasn't thinking because there wasn't any time to think. If I had lived life in a vacuum, maybe I could have continued indefinitely.

On October 10 I received a call from my lawyer, Gerhard Strate, in Germany. I'd hired a private attorney to work with the prosecutor on the Parche case. Strate's job was to make sure everything went correctly and that my interests were taken into account. Strate had called to tell me that Günther Parche was going to be tried in three days — for "bodily injury."

Bodily injury? The guy had tried to kill me: why wasn't he being tried for attempted murder? My lawyer said that because there were conflicting witness reports — eleven out of twelve witnesses said that Parche attempted to stab me twice; one claimed he only struck once and made no move to stab again — the German court, under law, had no choice but to believe the witness that favored the accused. Parche's statement that he'd wanted to wound me, not kill me, coupled with one testimony saying that he hadn't been prepared to stab me a second time, was enough to get him off the hook for attempted murder. Why, I wondered, was the court prepared to believe everything Parche said? And why was I being put on the defensive?

I was still certain that Parche would be convicted and receive jail time. He'd either be sent to prison or a mental institution.

"Monica, I think you're wrong," Zoltan told me during the trial. "I think that guy is going to walk free. Be prepared."

"No way, Zoltan," I disagreed. I'd been told that Parche's original idea was to give me some flowers in the hotel lobby and then cut off my hands. A guy like that wouldn't be set free. No way.

Thousands of witnesses had seen him attack me. That was good, because there was no way I was going to go back to Hamburg to testify during the trial. I would have had to sit at the prosecutor's table with my back to Parche. I just couldn't do that. So I stayed in Sarasota, trained hard, and tried not to think about the verdict.

On October 13, 1993, my mother and I were walking through an outdoor shopping area in Florida when we saw Zoltan running toward us.

"He's free," Zoltan said.

My brother didn't need to say a name. "He's free" was enough. "You're kidding me," I said as I stared into Zoltan's face.

"He'll spend tonight in jail because the court is worried about his safety. But tomorrow he'll walk out a free man — he can go anywhere in the world."

I sat down on the curb and let Zoltan's words sink in. And then I began to laugh. This was a black comedy. "Tell me how," I said when my uncontrollable giggles had subsided.

"We expect that the accused will not do anything punishable in the future." That is what the judge said when she handed down Günther Parche's sentence. Parche was found guilty of attempted bodily injury and given two years' probation instead of the maximum five years in prison. Parche's defender had previously warned the court that additional imprisonment would "destroy" his client. What about the prison I now lived in? I thought in shock as Zoltan explained the verdict. He gets to go free and I have to live in fear?

The judge partially blamed "star hype" and the media for Parche becoming a fanatical Graf fan, Zoltan explained. She declared that Steffi Graf only came into the small world of Parche through radio and television. Before his obsession with Steffi, Parche had lived happily. What did that have to do with anything?

"If every murderer said that, before their obsession with their ex-wife, brother, or boss, they had lived happily, would they get off with two years' probation after a murderous attack, too?" I asked Zoltan and my mother. They had no answer. "Tell me the rest," I said tiredly.

Zoltan said that the judge also based her decision on the fact that "The confession was absolutely believable," and that Parche had disclosed his motives from the start. According to the judge the "monstrous press reports," had been punishment enough for the accused. As for the decision to indict Parche on charges of bodily injury instead of attempted murder, that was blamed on conflicting witness reports and on my not releasing my physicians from their duty of confidentiality. And the witnesses who saw Parche stab me? Their statements were taken, but not one was called to testify during the trial.

"It seems that the Judge already knew everything she needed to know before the trial began," Zoltan added.

"And what about the psychiatrist's report that stated Parche had a 'serious personality disorder,'" I asked.

Zoltan explained that at the trial the psychiatrist had softened his original diagnosis. "He wanted to help Steffi Graf," the psychiatrist claimed. "He only wanted to give Monica Seles something to think about because she had driven Steffi Graf from number one in the world rankings."

I'd spend the next two years in the jail he was supposed to inhabit. Two years hiding in shadows, afraid to play professional tennis, afraid to even step onto a public court. And the man with a "serious personality disorder," would be free on probation with no court order for psychological counseling.

There was nothing we could do but file an appeal for a retrial. There was nothing the world could do, but join in my own shock.

The WTA Tour Players Association released the following statement:

The decision announced today by the German court in the Monica Seles stabbing incident is deplorable and shocking. We consider it outrageous that someone could commit a premeditated attack, inflict bodily harm and essentially get away with it. This man viciously attacked Monica in a life-threatening manner and has escaped punishment. The players and the entire tennis community are in shock over the judicial decision announced earlier today. We would expect that the prosecutor will appeal against the court's decision to the full extent allowable by German law.

Newspapers around the world published the following editorial comments:

. . . Germany is behind the US in identifying hate crimes, sex crimes, stalking and the like. But not so far behind in their perpetration. Günther Parche reportedly spent his first night of freedom locked up in jail for his own safety at his own request. He understands what he did better than did the judge.

. . . Parche is a proven crackpot (you have to hope someone in his family or his acquaintance will prevail upon him to seek psychiatric help). The Judge's handling of this case has shed light — again — on the German judicial system's peculiar and lax response to recent nationalistic or terroristic violence. That a woman judge presided over Parche's case proves nothing, either, except women can be just as stupid as men.

Günther Parche has attained his goal; Steffi Graf is once again at the top. The sole, horrifying question which one can ask, is: How will Parche react when his "goddess" is shaken from her pedestal?

Psychotherapist Stefan Larmer commented: "The decision contains a contradiction. The man is considered to be mentally disturbed enough to mitigate the punishment, but apparently not disturbed enough to require therapy."

Various tennis players also expressed shock: Anke Huber said: "I am very surprised by the decision. It is unfair and scandalous. One simply can't feel at home on the court."

Martina Navratilova: "You guys need some serious help with the laws here in Germany."

Chris Evert: "It seems like the whole thing was finally disappearing, but now it's being dredged up again. It's terrible for [Monica's] peace of mind, especially now that she was starting to prepare for a comeback."

"Can I have the car keys?" I said to Zoltan as I stood up from the curb. He handed me the keys and I walked away from my family. That day I drove and drove without stopping. "Why?" I screamed in the silence of the car. "Why–Why–Why!" I cried until my eyes were so swollen it was hard to see the road. I yelled until my voice was hoarse. When I returned home near midnight, my family was waiting for me in the kitchen.

"Don't ever do that again," my mother cried when I came into the house. "We were worried!"

"I'm sorry," I said softly. "I just need to think about this alone." That night I went to my room and tried to remember a time when my biggest fear was facing a tough opponent on the tennis court.

18

I was nervous. I knew after the Italian Open that I could play great tennis. But back in May of 1990 I was set to play Steffi Graf in the finals of the Lufthansa Cup. Steffi Graf, last time we'd competed, had sent me off the court at Wimbledon with my tail between my legs.

We were playing in Germany — Steffi's homeland. Spectators at the 1990 German Open tournament were not only bursting with pride for their compatriot; they were Germans finally unified. I remember that both the East and West German presidents were at the tournament finals (I took advantage of being in Berlin during that time and visited the Berlin Wall — I still have a piece at home). East and west, all cheering for a German. Still, the fans were very fair, and cheered for us both equally.

I let my worries slide away and concentrated on the match. I won the first set, 6–4. All I could think was that I'd taken a set from Steffi, and maybe she wouldn't trounce me in forty minutes. When I won the second set, 6–3, I was as shocked as the rest of the world. Nobody had expected me to beat Steffi — she was the unbeatable one. I went to the net to shake Steffi's hand. "Good match," I said.

My father has always stressed sportsmanship to me. If I win or lose, it's the same. He taught me that by example. When I look to the stands after a tough point, he is cheering. It doesn't matter who won the point, he claps anyway. While he'd love his daughter to win, he appreciates good tennis and rewards the victor. His actions are genuine. "Tennis is a game," he has often told me. "It is only a small part of life, Monica. Love, marriage, family, friends, that is what matters."

The award presentation at the German Open was surreal. The crowd cheered for me, but they were still in shock. The media people had to reorganize themselves because they thought Steffi would win. In the locker room after the ceremony I sat down and let the fact that I'd finally beaten Steffi Graf sink in. My thoughts were interrupted when Steffi entered the locker room. She took her racket and slammed it into the wall. It made a huge hole.

I had never seen anyone that unhappy after losing a match. At the Italian Open Martina had come up and congratulated me on my game. At the Lufthansa Cup Steffi never talked to me. I felt bad that I could do that to another person. I'd always thought that tennis was only a game — may the better player win. And, in the future, Steffi did beat me many times. To this day, I keep remembering Steffi hitting a hole in the wall. When I'm disappointed after a match, I look at my racket and think, this is only a game . . . and the game isn't me.

On to the 1990 French Open at Roland Garros Stadium.

When Betsy Nagelsen asked me to be her doubles partner at the French Open, I agreed. As always, the chance to have fun with Betsy outweighed the drawbacks — late nights and fatigue. Little did I know then that my decision would so anger a former doubles partner that she'd almost eliminate me in singles at the Open.

Her name was Helen Kelesi. In the past we'd played doubles together. We'd won some and lost some, and all in all we were pretty good partners. Still, there was no spoken or unspoken agreement that we'd play together exclusively. At least I didn't think so. But when I teamed up with Betsy, Helen was furious. And, as luck would have it, she was my second-round singles opponent.

It was the last match of the day. Helen and I walked to the court in silence, but before we started we spoke briefly at the net. Helen explained not too kindly that she was planning on destroying me for choosing Betsy as a doubles partner. To say I was surprised at her anger would be putting it mildly. Helen is a very competitive person, but I couldn't believe my decision had made her so mad: mad enough to play off the wall.

Helen won the first set, 6–4. "Great, now I have to win the next two," I mumbled. I fought back and won the second, 6–4. I was one up, and the look on Helen's face told me that she was ready to do battle. She wanted to beat me so badly that even I could taste it! In the end I pulled off the third set, 6–4. What a relief!

Meanwhile, Betsy and I made it to the third round of the doubles tournament. Even though we lost, I was still glad I'd played with her. I turned my focus back to singles. Two wins later, I'd made it to the quarterfinals.

"Monica doesn't know how to play tennis. Let's see how she does when she gets older." That's just one of the comments I've heard Manuela Maleeva of Bulgaria make about me over the years. Manuela is the eldest of the three Maleeva sisters, all tennis players. In 1990 Manuela was a top ten player. I can only assume that she felt threatened by my rise in the ranks.

In the past I'd beaten Manuela repeatedly. It always surprised me to hear the negative comments she made after our matches. She just couldn't say: "Monica played some good tennis."

Manuela took the first set, 3–6, and I won the second, 6–1. She was leading 4–1 in the third when, out of the blue, she called an injury time out, claiming that she had done something to her leg. It was very strange: I hadn't seen anything that would have made her claim credible. She hadn't tripped, or leapt for a wide shot. She just wanted me to think she wasn't at her best — to play with my mind.

I couldn't understand Manuela's logic: the momentum was on her side and she had me right where she wanted me. A few minutes later she came back onto the court. Maybe she thought I'd be unnerved by the break in action. Instead, her stunt made me more focused. And when I'm concentrating, I'm twice as powerful. I'm going to win this match, I thought. I took the third set, 7–5. On to the semifinals.

* * *

"The battle of two children." That's what the press called my semifinal match against Jennifer Capriati. And we were just kids — sixteen- and fourteen-year-olds caught up in a media event wired with electricity. It was the first time we'd played each other, and neither of us knew what to expect.

Jennifer had only played two major tournaments before the French Open. And, though she'd done unbelievably well, the hype and pressure of the semifinals rattled her.

I can't explain how strange it is to be a child and have people labeling you after a ten-minute interview. "Tough, tenacious, mentally strong" — that's what the press had labeled me. And now Jennifer, whose personality was even less formed than mine, was facing the same situation. Even more bizarre, I was the more seasoned player in the face of pressure. It seemed only yesterday that I'd watched Chris Evert remain poised and confident at her last US Open, while I crumbled in a crackle of nerves. I won the French Open semis against Jennifer in a fairly easy match, 6–2, 6–2.

I faced Steffi Graf in the finals. I want this, I thought as I stepped onto the court. I want to win in this great stadium — the one I dreamed about as a child.

I was up 3–0 in the first set when rain forced Steffi and me off the court. During a delay, most players talk with their coaches. It's really their only legal opportunity: coaches and players aren't allowed to communicate during a match, although many do. My father and I don't do that. Nor do we talk during rain delays. Both my dad and I believe that coaches are valuable in practice, but during a match, I'm the only one that matters.

After forty minutes, Steffi and I returned to the court. I was disappointed that the delay had lasted so long. I'd had momentum in my favor before the rain came down. Now it was like beginning the match again. Steffi played hard, and tied us 3 all. The next few games were so even that we ended up 6 all in the first set and had to play a tie-breaker.

Tie-breakers are so short that one mistake can cost a player the set. I've always believed that, unlike a match, tie-breakers are about luck. With two even players, it can go either way. Steffi had me 6–2 in the tie-breaker, needing only one more point to win the set. I fought until we were tied 6–6 — a startling comeback. The tension in the stadium was incredible. Fans could barely stay in their seats as we prepared to fight for the points left to take the set. The final point went my way. I breathed more than relief out.

The momentum shifted my way. I'd won the first set, and deep down I knew I had a good chance of winning the second. You can do this, Monica, I thought; stay focused, you can do this. I took the second set 6–4. And as I ran to the net to shake a silent Steffi's hand, it hit me that I'd just won my first Grand Slam title. At sixteen years and six months, I'd become the youngest player to win a Grand Slam singles event since Lottie Dod won Wimbledon in 1887 at fifteen years, ten months.

Grand Slam titles are very special to tennis players: they put you up with the very few at the top. It's a kind of rite of passage — winning the French Open told me that I'd finally made it. I no longer had to wonder whether I was good enough, or chalk up my wins to luck. I had made it, and nobody could take that away from me.

19

"Everything is too simple in tennis now. Wouldn't it be neat to bring high fashion back to the sport? To be like Suzanne [Lenglen], like Madonna?" I was barely sixteen when I told a reporter that one of my favorite singers was Madonna and that my favorite old player was Lenglen. For the last six years I've had to live with those words. Journalists are still asking me which of Madonna's songs are my new favorites, and whether or not I know that Suzanne Lenglen died unhappy, and young. So now is my chance to set things straight. And I'm going to take it.

First, I think Madonna is great. At that time she was one of my favorite singers. She was different, exciting, a rebel. I still like her music, but I like countless other musicians as well — nobody has just one favorite artist.

Now Suzanne: in 1919 Suzanne Lenglen knocked the tennis establishment on its ear. She was graceful, daring, and more athletic on the court than any other woman in the sport. Suzanne played her first tournament when she was twelve, and by the time she'd reached fifteen, she'd won the World Hard Court Championships. She was the Michael Jordan of tennis: racing across the court to turn unbelievable gets into winners, leaping for shots, and making contact with both feet in the air, Suzanne was a powerful dynamo at a time when women were supposed to be passive and ladylike. I've always wished I could hit a shot with two feet in the air, like Suzanne.

But she did more for women's tennis than win. She was great friends with Ted Tinling — known as "The Leaning Tower of Pizzaz," because he was six foot five inches tall, with a shiny bald head and a style all

his own. He was a benefactor of tennis, an umpire and master of ceremonies for women's matches in the twenties, including some of
Suzanne's, and later in life he became a clothing designer.

In the late 1920s Ted began designing dresses for Suzanne. The first
dress she wore at Wimbledon came just below her knee, and the sleeves
barely reached past her elbows. Up until then women had been wearing
ankle-length skirts, blouses with corsets, and long sleeves. The dress
created almost as much controversy as Suzanne did by drinking cognac
during the changeovers.

When I joined the tour, Ted Tinling befriended me. At the time, he
was minister of protocol and the announcer for Virginia Slims tournaments. He told me all about Suzanne — about the power of her game,
her dresses, and her father, who was obsessed with his daughter's tennis
career. When she was a child, he drilled her hour after hour on the
court. Even after she became a tennis star, he constantly harassed her
on and off the court. When I heard those stories, I'd think about my
dad. I was lucky.

People who knew Suzanne say that she was a pretty unhappy young
woman; that her father drove her to the edge of health and sanity, and
that her own personality allowed her to step over. Suzanne died at
thirty-nine of pernicious anemia. Still, when I was sixteen, I was fasci-
nated by Suzanne. She was the first high fashion tennis player: her
outfits on court were beautiful, and I'd still like to play a match in
dresses like hers. Her behavior off the court was said to be even more
daring than her fashions: I've never wanted to emulate her in that way,
but I'll always admire her strength, spirit, and dynamic athleticism.

I think that Ted Tinling contributed a lot to my fascination with
Suzanne. First, I'd always loved designing dresses. As a kid, I'd pore
over fashion magazines and get my mother to help me create new outfits.
By the time I met Mr. Tinling, he was a respected designer — couturier
for the Virginia Slims circuit. I loved talking to him about the dresses
he created, and he always seemed to have time to talk to me.

He was like that — a truly gentle, kind man. He was an advocate for women's tennis long before anyone really paid attention to us. I think he was in love with Suzanne Lenglen a long time ago. Perhaps that's what made me love her, too.

Ted Tinling died on May 23, 1990, in Cambridge, England. He was seventy-nine years old. Most of the women players were still in France for the Open. However, we were told by the tournament director that there would be a memorial just before the start of Wimbledon. That way we'd be given the opportunity to pay tribute to Ted Tinling.

Sadly, I only saw a couple of women players there. It struck me that so many people had spoken about Ted, said great things about him, but none of them had bothered to come to his funeral.

If Suzanne Lenglen had been alive, she would have been there.

20

I can't be sure, but I think Suzanne Lenglen would have appreciated the humor in the situation. And I certainly wasn't above laughing at myself. If I had been, 1990 Wimbledon would have been an ordeal.

The Grunt-o-Meter was unveiled during my first-round match there. It was a device designed by a reporter for a London tabloid to measure the exact decibel level of my grunts. Eighty-two decibels — that's the level of noise they recorded, placing my grunts somewhere between a "pneumatic drill and a diesel train." I actually thought the entire exercise was funny. It had nothing to do with tennis, but I saw the humor.

Everybody grunts — Gaby Sabatini, Anke Huber, Jennifer Capriati. I'm probably the loudest, at least according to the Grunt-o-Meter, but I didn't realize how loudly I was grunting until I watched a tape of myself on television. My grunts have always been a natural way to release air and energy. Any athlete who exerts momentary bursts of physical effort has to release the air in her lungs. In the junior tournaments I played, we all grunted. But I wasn't in the juniors anymore; I was at Wimbledon.

I was still on a streak: six major tournament wins in 1990, my first Grand Slam title. Since I was playing well, and the tabloids had nothing to write about me, they focused intensely on the grunting. I wasn't engaged, had no illicit affairs with married men, no drinking or drug habits — what else was there? Like any joke, it was funny once; even twice. But repeated too many times, it began to taste bitter. I realized that the grunting issue wasn't the harmless joke I'd imagined. It was a ploy by the media to create something negative about me. Controversy sells papers.

Later in my career, newspapers worldwide would promote me as "The Grunting Monica — watch her and hear for yourself how noisy she is!" I was disappointed that the grunting issue blew up into an ugly attraction and controversy. Still, there was nothing I could do but play.

I think it's particularly frustrating for athletes — as opposed to celebrities — to read about themselves in tabloids. We don't go into our sport because we want to be famous. We begin to play tennis, or hockey, or track and field, because we love the sport. Fame isn't the primary goal. I understand, now, that it comes with the territory. But that's a lesson hard learned.

"Monica is obsessed with butter." That was one of the more amusing things written about me that year in London. I told a reporter that I liked butter, and he wrote that I couldn't live without it — that I put it on pizza, desserts, everything. "Monica is addicted to butter," he claimed. I mean, come on! Later, the stories would get nastier, more personal. Had I known just how hurtful the media could be, I would have laughed more in 1990. As it was, I tried to keep a sense of humor while dealing with the fallout created by the tabloids.

"I would readily relax the all-white clothes rule if I could just get rid of the grunts," a high-ranked Wimbledon official was quoted as saying in the press. When I read that quote, I had the uncomfortable feeling that the media has accomplished their goal. They'd found something negative about my game, and now anyone who didn't like me was ready to jump on the "ban grunting" bandwagon.

Players began to complain — mostly to the media, occasionally on the court. Nobody had cared that I grunted in 1988 or 1989, but in 1990, I was winning. I was third in the world — a real threat to the top players. And some of them were willing to use anything to disrupt my concentration. Still, it wasn't as bad as it would be in 1992. After all, I wasn't number one, yet.

I'm not sure whether the media attention affected my game, I was tired from the French Open, or I was just off. Regardless, when it was time to play Zina Garrison in the quarterfinals, I wasn't the best player on the court. Zina played a great match and beat me, 3–6, 6–3, 9–7. It had been close. Zina kept missing her inside forehand shot all three sets, but at match point she hit a forehand blast right down the line. I saw the white dust from the line spring into the air, and there was no doubt I'd just lost the match.

If I'm going to lose, I like to see that the final point was owned by my opponent. There was no doubt that Zina's forehand was right down the line. But that's not always the case. There are tournaments where line calls decide who has won a match, and they're not always right.

In 1989 I played a finals match against Mary Joe Fernandez in Germany. Mary Joe was up 5–1, and I fought back to 6 all. During a tie-breaker in the third set, I was up 3–1 and hit what I believe was a good shot. The umpire called my ball out. I went over to him and tried to argue the point. I was overruled, and the point went to Mary Joe. That meant that the tie-breaker score was 3–2, Seles. But when I went back to the baseline, the umpire called out 4–1, Fernandez.

There are only seven points in a tie-breaker: every single one matters. In a split second, the umpire had taken away two from me and given them to Mary Joe. The crowds began to boo. I called for the tournament director, who came out but had no idea what had happened, because she hadn't been there for the point. The match wasn't televised, so there was no way to check what had occurred. I lost the tie-breaker and the match.

My loss to Zina Garrison at Wimbledon ended my six-tournament streak. Zina faced Steffi in the semifinals and won, 6–3, 3–6, 6–4, but lost to Martina in the finals. Meanwhile, I returned to the States to get ready for the US Open.

"Are you sure?" my father asked.

"Yes, it just feels right," I replied as I swung my new Yonex racket.

My father was concerned. Switching rackets mid-season, and so close to a Grand Slam tournament, isn't the norm for a player. Usually, it takes months to get used to a new racket. Players like Courier and

Sampras won't switch racket brands, no matter how much money they're offered. I'd been happy with my old racket, but when I picked up the Yonex, I knew within five minutes that the racket had been made for me. The unique shape and mid-size fit my game perfectly, giving me both power and control.

I played my first match with the new racket just two and a half weeks after I'd picked it up. I beat Martina in the finals of Virginia Slims in Los Angeles. That win gave me the confidence to take it to the US Open.

My first and second rounds at the Open went easily. Third round, I played Linda Ferrando of Italy. The match was at 11:00 am, and I remember I was a bit worried. I'd never played Linda, so I didn't know what to expect. It was a sunny, hot day, and as a left hander, I found serving difficult because of the orientation of center court. Still, I took the first set, 6–1.

Everything was going well. I was up 40–love, first serve of the second set. Linda fought back to 40–30. Take control, I told myself. Linda hit me an easy overhead and I looked up, ready to put it away and take the first game. I couldn't see it! The glare of the sun blinded me, and I felt dizzy as I tried to find the yellow velvet spot in the orange blaze. What an idiot you are, Monica, I thought angrily as I watched my shot fall into the net.

I don't know if I lost all my confidence, or Linda found hers, but she took the second set, 6–1. In the third set, I couldn't get a ball into her court. Everything I hit missed the line, went wide, long, into the net. I couldn't get that easy overhead out of my mind, couldn't focus on taking control. Linda took the third, 7–6, in a huge upset. I was ranked third in the world, and I was out of the 1990 US Open in the third round.

Too many excuses. That's what I thought to myself as I collected my rackets and walked off the court. The sun had been too bright, the day too hot, my opponent unknown. Too many excuses, and none of them made up for the fact that I'd lost. I was disappointed with myself — I hadn't tried hard enough.

The following morning I was scheduled to play doubles. When I arrived at the court, it was surrounded by journalists. They thought I might not show up because I'd lost my singles match in the third round. It was weird — why wouldn't I show up for my match? Yes, I'd lost, and I was embarrassed by the way I'd played. But tennis is a game, and in games someone wins and someone loses. That's just the way it goes.

I may have lost at the Open, but I was still ranked third in the world. I'd qualified for the Virginia Slims Championships at Madison Square Gardens. I went, determined to play better than the previous year; determined to try to get one more game, one more set, one round further.

That championship is the only women's tournament in the world where we play the best of five sets: in order to win, we've got to take three, just like the men. I love the format. It's fun to play like the men — to spend hours out on the court sweating it out with your opponent.

In 1990 I made it to the finals and faced Gabriela Sabatini. Gaby is a strong top-spin, back-court player. She's an all-round tough opponent, and she'd beaten Steffi that year to make it to the finals. I took the first set, 6–4. Gaby fought back and took the second and third, 7–5, 6–3, which meant that I had to take the next two sets to win.

We'd been playing almost three hours by the time the fourth set began. I want this — I really want this, I thought. I took the next set, 6–4. We were tied two sets apiece, and about to play the first five-set women's match since the 1901 Nationals. Later, the media would write that "A new day had begun" in women's tennis. I didn't know anything about a new day at the time. All I wanted was to take the fifth set. Four hours into the match, I did, 6–2.

It didn't matter to me that I'd become the youngest player ever to win a Virginia Slims Championship. What mattered was that in the game of tennis, this time I'd played my best.

$$\left(21\right)$$

I felt as if I was on an express train to the top of women's tennis, and I was still riding the wave of the Virginia Slims Championship when I flew to the Australian Open in January 1991. I dropped only twelve games in the first five rounds there. My momentum built as I defeated Anke Huber in the quarterfinals.

By the time I reached my semifinal match against Mary Joe Fernandez, I knew I was playing great tennis. We started at noon. The sun beat down on the outdoor surface, and its heat rebounded off the court. Despite the rising temperature, I took the first set from Mary Joe, 6–3.

One hundred and thirty-four degrees: that's what the thermometer read as we began our second set. I'd never played in that type of heat. The Australian stadium was set fairly low, and I felt as if I was running through thick, steaming air. In 1991 there were no water-break rules at the Australian Open (now there's a ten-minute break after one set apiece). The soles of my feet began to burn and ache. That night, I would discover blisters stretching the entire length of my foot. Mary Joe began playing very well, and I lost the second set, 6–love.

The third set was extremely difficult. Mary Joe had me 7–6 in the third and we played her match point. It was a long one. You don't want to play long for the match — it's much too nerve-racking. I finally put the ball away. We were tied, 7–7.

The only Grand Slam tournament where there's a tie-breaker in the third set is the US Open. Even though I was overheated and exhausted, I was glad there would be no tie-breaker to end our match. As I've said before, tie-breakers are like Russian roulette. You get two equal players, and it's just a question of luck. I was able to break Mary Joe the next game, and then went on to win the match 9–7. There was just no liquid left in my body — I'd sweated it all out.

The day of the Australian Open finals was cool. Well, not exactly cool, but at least it was only 105 degrees. My opponent, Jana Novotna, took the first set, 5–7. I rallied and won the second, 6–3. Here we go again, I thought as we began the third. I was worried that it would be another long one. Thankfully, I took it, 6–1. I'd won my first Australian Open Grand Slam.

There wasn't much time to celebrate. I flew to Japan for the Pan Pacific Open. It was a long way to go for nothing. I had to default after a doubles match because I was sick. After spending two weeks in the heat of Australia, and running down my body in long matches, I just wasn't ready for the cold weather in Tokyo. I returned to Florida to recuperate.

I needed all my strength for the Lipton Championship in Miami. I beat Gaby in the finals in two sets. But that wasn't the most memorable thing about the tournament. Jennifer Capriati and I played in the quarterfinals, and it was a really tough match. We slugged it out in three sets, and I won 2–6, 6–1, 6–4. I have rarely been so exhausted after a match. Jennifer and I ran each other to the ends of the earth. After it was over, we hugged. I was so beat, I could hardly walk off the court.

I went on to San Antonio for the US Hardcourt Championships. Steffi and I faced each other in the finals. It was a strange match — not because I didn't play my best, or because Steffi beat me in two sets. It was strange, because at that point it was only a matter of weeks before I would replace Steffi as the number one player in the world. A few weeks earlier, Steffi had lost to Gaby at the finals in Boca Raton. That loss, coupled with my win at the Australian Open, moved my point ranking higher than Steffi's. It was enough to end her 1,310-day reign as number one.

After San Antonio I realized that Steffi and I were embarking on a relationship not unlike Chris Evert and Martina's. We would play against each other on center courts around the world. Our rivalry would be big business, a big draw. In the past, we'd battled it out on the courts, but I'd always been number two or three. Never had I sat on the number one throne, which for so long had been Steffi's. Never, until March 11, 1991.

I did not become number one until after a March Virginia Slims tournament in Palm Springs, California. There was a lot of press-driven pressure there, which was difficult to ignore. I understood that becoming the youngest woman ever to be ranked number one was big news. In addition, Steffi had been considered invincible. To replace her as number one player, at seventeen, was a shocker. But it didn't happen in Palm Springs.

The way it worked, if I played a top-five player in the finals of the Palm Springs tournament and won, I'd instantly move into the number one slot. Beating a top player would have given me the necessary bonus points to change my rank immediately. If I lost, I'd have to wait a week until Steffi's results dropped off and I was given points for my past few wins.

It rained through most of the outdoor tournament. While we waited for it to stop, I trained as much as I could. On the Saturday before my first match my mother came running up to me as I hit, something small and brown held in her hands.

"Astro has been bitten!" she cried. I looked down at her hands and saw my Yorkshire Terrier curled in a tiny ball.

"What happened?" I asked.

"A big dog without a collar or leash attacked him," Mom explained through her tears. "He took Astro in his mouth and shook him back and forth, then dropped him."

Astro wasn't moving. I grabbed my bag and we raced to the veterinary emergency room. My dog remained curled up in a ball, shaking. Astro's whole personality, his ego, seemed crushed. He is a tiny dog, but he thinks he's the king of the jungle. In a split second, he'd learned the truth. The emergency room stitched him up, and we took him back to the hotel.

By the next night, we all thought Astro was dying. "We've got to do something," I said to my mother. I was about to play in an important tournament, and all I could think about was my dog. I grabbed the yellow pages and called every vet clinic in the book. I finally found one open twenty-four hours a day.

We drove in the darkness and rain, Astro still curled up on my mother's lap. The vet told us that he had a very high temperature. He'd developed an infection from the bite, and was weak because he'd lost a lot of blood. She said he was very sick, and that we should leave him at the clinic. I was sure I'd never see my dog again.

The next morning the rain stopped. Since the forecast predicted more to come, the tournament was packed into two days — two matches on Saturday, two on Sunday. I hardly remember playing; all I could think about was my dog. I made it to the finals, then lost to Martina. The press would have to wait a week before they printed that I was number one.

After my match I raced to the veterinary clinic. Astro had improved. He could come home with me.

I did a telephone interview that night. The reporter asked if I was disappointed that I wouldn't be number one for a week. I turned and looked over at Astro, lying on a big cushion at my side. I thought about telling him about my dog, named after the dog in "The Jetsons" cartoon — Astro, who never cared whether or not I'd had a bad loss; whether practice had gone well, or poorly. Astro, who couldn't read untrue articles about me in the tabloids, and wouldn't have cared if he could; who thought I was number one, regardless of rank. Astro was just happy to see me, day in day out. Losing him would have meant losing a normality in my life that I cherish. Astro, like my family, loves me no matter what, and I need that. I told the reporter that I wasn't terribly disappointed.

Being number one has never been a goal for me. My goal has always been to do well at Grand Slams. A rank is just a number on a piece of paper, but when you win a Grand Slam, there is so much excitement and emotion. Somehow, it's anti-climactic to hold a ranking list; holding up a trophy before a stadium of cheering fans, now that's thrilling. I'm not saying that becoming number one wasn't an honor. It meant that I was the best in my sport, and that's incredible. But I think it meant more to the media than it did to me.

In the end, what changed the most when I became number one was the media requests. Previously, I'd done some magazine articles and a few interviews. When I became number one, the requests poured in. People wanted me on their television shows, in their newspapers, at their parades.

Everyone wanted to know how it felt to be the youngest number one player in history. I tried to explain that it felt great, but that it was something I hadn't aimed to achieve. I'd worked hard from age six because I loved the game of tennis. Becoming number one was just a bonus.

22

Before I left for the May 1991 French Open, I signed with Matrix hair care company to endorse their products. They wanted me to cut my hair. The last time I'd had short hair was when I was thirteen, and it had been quite an adjustment for a gangly little girl. I remember riding a bus in Novi Sad; a man who wanted the seat beside me said, "Move over, little boy." I hadn't cut my hair since. But Matrix was my new sponsor, and I wanted them to be happy. I was also ready for a change.

The whole experience was exciting and fun. I sat in the salon chair and let the stylist cut my pony-tail off in one snip. I posed for pictures, my thick locks in my hand. Then the stylist went to work and gave me a short, fashionable cut for Paris. I loved it!

In Paris I tried to forget my new look and focus on the Open. I had won it the previous year, and wanted a repeat performance. I moved through my first few rounds with ease, and found myself facing Gabriela Sabatini in the semifinals. I defeated Gaby, 6–4, 6–1, in a straightforward match. My game was right on, and I was ready to play Steffi Graf in the finals.

It didn't happen. Steffi lost in the semis to Arantxa Sanchez Vicario, 6–0, 6–2. It was the fewest games won by Steffi in a match since 1982. Arantxa and I played in the finals, which I won in two sets, 6–3, 6–4. That made me only the third player in the era of the Open to capture a French and Australian Open in the same calendar year.

I was thrilled to have won a second consecutive French Open, and excited at the prospect of returning to Wimbledon and trying for the finals. My tennis career was hurtling forward, and I felt nothing could stop me — nothing, but a painful bump on my left shin which I'd assumed would go down a few days after the French finals. Instead, it got worse. When I tried to run in my sneakers, sharp pains shot up and down my leg.

The worst part was that it was my fault. I had been jogging on pavement for the last few weeks to lose the weight I'd gained. The impact had given me shin splints. In addition, during my semifinals match I'd hit my left leg with my racket, which aggravated the problem.

I went to see Dr. Steadman, who happened to be in Paris for the Open. He told me that I needed to rest my leg and that, if the inflammation went down, I could play at Wimbledon. I returned to Florida to rest. A week went by, and the bump on my leg was still there. Just touching it hurt. Still, I didn't call the WTA to pull out of Wimbledon. I wanted to play. The idea of missing a Grand Slam event, disappointing the fans and myself, was hard to swallow. I flew to Dr. Steadman's clinic in Vail. Maybe he could make my leg heal more quickly. I didn't imagine, at that point, that if I pulled out of Wimbledon, there'd be more than a few lines in the paper. I hadn't accepted that from the moment I became number one, almost everything I did would be of interest to the media.

My brother came with me to Vail. He watched as I tried to get my leg working; watched as the pain increased, because what my leg needed was rest.

"Monica, it's not working," he said finally. "You've got to take some time off to heal."

"Maybe if I just work a little harder," I suggested. "Maybe then I can play . . ."

I was torn. I really wanted to play Wimbledon: I had a shot at joining Steffi Graf to become the second female Grand Slam title winner (Australia, France, Wimbledon, and the US Open) in three years. Only a handful of women in the history of the sport have ever had that honor. But physically, I knew I couldn't play.

Zoltan called my manager, Stephanie Tolleson, and told her that I was having a hard time making the decision. He said she should go ahead and pull me out of Wimbledon, because it was getting so late. Stephanie called me, and I told her to wait. I just couldn't accept the reality of the situation. Three days before the June tournament began, Zoltan told Stephanie to release a statement saying that "due to an injury caused by a minor accident," I would have to pull out of Wimbledon.

My tabloid quotient soared. There I was in Vail getting physical therapy — pretty boring stuff — and the tabloids were writing things like I was pregnant. Wow, I thought, my life is a lot more exciting in the tabloids than it is in reality. They went so far as to say that I had been paid a $1million-dollar bonus by Yonex *not* to play in the Grand Slam! It was out of control — and none of it was true. I was in Vail getting physical therapy for what turned out to be the beginning of a stress fracture in my left leg, and the press was going nuts. I wasn't trying to be elusive. I was focusing on my therapy, and honestly didn't know about the fuss until Zoltan flew to Vail and told me.

"Why would I miss Wimbledon? It's the only Grand Slam I haven't won," I said to my brother in shock. "Why are they making all these things up?"

"It's none of their business, anyway," Zoltan said. "You've done everything by the rules." He was upset at the way the press and especially the tabloids in London were treating his little sister. Meanwhile, my father was saying we shouldn't be angry at the press. He was a journalist for thirty-five years and he understood their love of sensational stories. "That's part of their job, Monica," he tried to explain.

I've always had a bit more trouble with London papers. The more upmarket ones have some of the best reporters in the world, and they do their homework. But there's no line the tabloids (both English and international) won't cross — even if it means renting a helicopter and flying over your home after you've been stabbed in the back, or going through your trash and climbing the wall outside your house when your father is trying to recuperate from a cancer operation.

"Don't even talk to the press. You don't need to justify your actions," Zoltan advised. "All you're trying to do is get healthy so you can play tennis without further injury — if they have a problem with that, too bad."

The tabloids began to pay people for information on my whereabouts. At one point, there was a $30,000 bounty for a photograph of me. But for some reason, no one could find me. If they hadn't assumed the worst, that I was lying; if they hadn't tried to make a story where there wasn't one, they'd have had no trouble. It seemed so obvious that I would be at a rehab clinic. But what was obvious to me wasn't obvious to the rest of the world.

I don't have to justify my decision to pull out of Wimbledon, I kept telling myself. I have a legitimate injury, I can't play — that should be the end of the discussion. Of course, it wasn't the end. When reporters began to hassle family friends to ferret out information, I finally said, enough.

"Zoltan, I need to talk to the media."

"You don't owe them anything," he replied.

"That's just the thing," I said sadly, "I do." I'd learned a tough lesson that June: I'd learned that being the number one tennis player in the world meant I had to explain my actions. If I pulled out of a match for physical reasons, I had to hold a press conference with my doctors to explain why. The media was responsible for keeping the fans informed. And the fans, by merit of their support for the game and for me, had earned the right to know. However, ultimately I believe that my private life should remain private. And in 1993, when my disappearance from the game was for both physical and intensely personal reasons, I would refuse to let the press in. Sometimes you just can't let everyone inside your mind.

The week after Wimbledon I was able to play in an exhibition in New Jersey. Unfortunately, the promoter arranged a major press conference and used me to promote the Mahwah, New Jersey, exhibition called the Pathmark Tennis Classic. He told me that the conference was a great opportunity to explain where I'd been the past month, but in reality he just wanted to generate publicity. Before the conference he gave me a

T-shirt to hold. I thought it was the same one he'd given me at the airport, which read, "Rome, Paris, Wimbledon, Mahwah." But the new T-shirt was different. It read, "Rome, Paris, Wimbledon, Mahwah" — but with Wimbledon crossed out.

The press conference was a zoo. Reporters asked about my supposed pregnancy and alleged insurance claims. "I'm sorry for the confusion," I said. "The truth is that I skipped Wimbledon because of shin splints and the beginning of a stress fracture in my left leg. People have been looking for more exciting answers — that I'm pregnant, that it's the Yonex contract. But why would I miss Wimbledon, the most prestigious tournament in the world, if I didn't have to?"

Only when I put all the rumors to rest did the press want to know about my left leg and physical therapy. When I had finished explaining, I held up the promoter's T-shirt for the photographers. I faced another barrage of questions. If I'd known the new shirt implied that I was thumbing my nose at Wimbledon, I would never have agreed to hold it. For weeks following the incident I received negative publicity.

Once again, I found myself apologizing. "No, I did not understand the shirt," I said over and over again. Never again would I agree to wear someone's shirt, or hold a sign for their business, so that they could snap a photo. I'd learned that everyone has a different agenda, and not all of them have my best interests at heart. I'm certain that the promoter didn't.

I thought that, after Mahwah, the fuss would die down. I was wrong.

I returned to the tour at the end of July. It had been a tough few months, and my game showed it. I went to a tournament in San Diego, and was upset by Jennifer Capriati. By the time the US Open came around, I'd begun to worry about my game. The press and the fans were hoping for a Graf vs. Seles final. I just hoped to avoid any further controversy and play good tennis.

And I did play well. I moved easily to the semifinals, giving up only one set in the first five rounds. My semi match was the last one of the day. Whoever won would have to return the next day to play in the finals. That's a tough schedule. If the match is long and difficult, it's hard to be fresh in less than twenty hours. But that's not what was on my mind that afternoon. I stood across the net from Jennifer Capriati. Jennifer had beaten me only a month earlier. My confidence wasn't at its peak.

The stands were jam-packed, and the crowd was rooting for Jennifer. She was the darling of tennis at that point — she had already been on the cover of *Sports Illustrated*, she was young, cute, and an American playing in the semis of the US Open. It was difficult to walk out on the court and hear most of the spectators cheering for Jennifer. I understood, but it was still hard.

The entire match was close — long points that went on and on, both of us hitting the ball so hard, both of us playing out of our minds. I took the first set, 6–3; Jennifer took the next, 3–6. We were tied, 1–1 going into the third and final set. The slug-fest continued. Jennifer had two chances to serve for the match in the third, but failed both times. I fought back until we were tied, 6 games apiece: a tie-breaker. Neither of us held serve until the eighth point. I pulled ahead, and took the third set with a 7–3 tie-breaker.

"Great playing," I said to Jennifer as we shook hands at the net. She smiled and nodded.

I went quickly to the press conference and did my interviews. I wanted to get out of the stadium and home to rest. Martina Navratilova had beaten Steffi Graf in their semifinal match, 7–6 (7–2), 6–7 (6–8), 6–4, and tomorrow I'd face her in the finals. If the scores from her semi match were any indication, Martina was playing great tennis. I'd need all my sleep that night.

Back at the hotel, I watched highlights from the day's matches to unwind. It was only then that I saw how upset Jennifer had been after our semifinals. Tears rolled down her face as she packed her bag and walked off the court. I understood. I would have cried after that match, too. Jennifer had been so close . . . it could have gone either way. I felt terrible that Jennifer was so sad, but I couldn't dwell on it because I had another match to play. And the bottom line, the thing I always told myself after hard losses, was that it was only a tennis game.

Another tie-breaker! Why all these tie-breakers, Monica? I asked myself as Martina and I prepared to fight for the first set of our US Open finals. All I could think was that maybe I wouldn't be as lucky as I'd been with Jennifer. Come on, Monica, I told myself, hold your serves this time. I won the tie-breaker, 7–1.

I was down love–40 in the first game of the second set when I heard Mayor Dinkins cheering for me in the stands. He helped me to find the spirit to fight back, and ultimately I took the second set, 6–1. I played some great tennis that afternoon, and only made five unforced errors to Martina's twenty-six. But most importantly, I'd won my first US Open. After my performance the previous year, I never thought I'd win the tournament. I let the fact that I'd taken three out of four Grand Slams in 1991 wash over me. It felt unbelievable.

The media were the first to point out that my third Grand Slam win must have felt bittersweet. "If you'd played Wimbledon, you might have joined the three women [Maureen Connolly, Margaret Smith Court, and Steffi Graf] who'd accomplished the rare feat of winning the four major championships in one year," they said. "Now you'll never know if you might have won the Grand Slam title."

They were right. I'd never know. But I couldn't change the fact that I'd been injured for Wimbledon. If I'd played, I wouldn't have won. And even if I had won, I might have injured myself further and ruined my season, or even my ability to play tennis in the future. Winning all four Grand Slams would have been incredible, but to do that takes an unbelievably consistent game of tennis. That's why only three women in the history of tennis have done it. Maybe I'll join their ranks in the future. Maybe not.

For all the might-have-beens, my US Open win was one of the most exciting moments in my life. What matters is playing the game well. What matters more is remembering that there's life after tennis. I want to live it without physical disabilities as a result of over-training, over-playing, and being over-obsessive.

In September I went on to Tokyo for the Nichirei International Ladies Championship. This time I didn't get sick, and was able to defeat Mary Joe Fernandez in the finals of the tournament. What I particularly liked about the championship was that, instead of a piece of crystal, the winner received a beautiful pendant. The sponsor is a company that makes cherry-flavored drinks, so the pendant has a ruby in it that's meant to look like a cherry. My pendant was beautiful, and whenever I wear it, I think about Tokyo and what a great time I had at the tournament.

When I returned to the United States, it was November. Time for the Virginia Slims Championships. There, I faced Martina Navratilova in the finals. Martina is a great athlete — maybe the best in the game. Every time I've played against her, I've been nervous. She has such an incredible reach that her opponent has to be able to judge passing shots very exactly.

The final of the '91 Slims was a tough one. I took the first set, 6–4; Martina rallied back to take the second, 3–6, which meant we had to play at least two more sets. I took the third in a close fight, 7–5. At that point I felt strong, my confidence was building, and I took the fourth set, 6–love. The win made me the seventh player ever to win ten or more tournaments in a single year.

It had been a great year for me. I had gained the confidence to withstand pressure, to face any opponent with the knowledge that I deserved to stand on the same court with her. I'd made mistakes that year: not talking immediately and directly to the media at Wimbledon was one of them; Mahwah was another. But I'd learned a lot, too. Unfortunately, there are no second chances as far as the media are concerned. The press would never again treat me with kid gloves. Maybe part of that was the fact that I'd turned eighteen.

Still, I've always enjoyed press conferences and interviews, and that hasn't changed to this day. Interviews give the fans a chance to see a side of me that they don't glimpse on the court, and allow me to develop some close ties with members of the press.

Lessons are a part of life, and I learned how to work with the press in 1991. Unfortunately, some lessons come even harder, and by 1993 I'd learnt that I could be blamed for just about anything . . . including playing great tennis. And that a man who was clearly unbalanced — who tried to kill me before 10,000 witnesses, wrote threatening letters to other athletes, and documented his obsession with Steffi Graf in letters, could be absolved of any crime.

$$\left(24\right)$$

The following letters were written by Günther Parche to the German athlete Heike Drechsler, and to Mrs. Graf and Steffi Graf. They were part of the police file compiled on Günther Parche.

"To Heike Drechsler

"Until today, I had quite a high opinion of you. For me, you were among the five best and most popular female athletes in Germany today. But now I am deeply disappointed and hurt. (See Neue Revue *No. 40 of September 25, 1992.) I bought it especially because I thought that those people on the radio had made a bad joke! I will not have anybody mention Stephanie Graf in connection with that dumb ape from Leimen, who can't speak German and should push off to Hafenstrasse in Hamburg or even better with Tiriac to Romania.*

"It may well be possible that some football players are earning too much (something should be done about that!). Stephanie Graf is the only person who really earned her millions (I would be glad to give her all my money). She is the most beautiful and wonderful thing on earth. For Stephanie, I would go through fire. Millions of people all over the world adore and love this beautiful young woman. The girl must have been sent to us from heaven. Stephanie's little finger is worth more than ten words from you.

"This was to make you think! Now you know that you made a mistake. I put it down to youthful exuberance.

'Anyone who dares to even touch Stephanie's reputation and honor must expect serious consequences."

From the New States

"*Dear Mrs. Graf,*

"*I have a small request. Your 'darling daughter' has her birthday on June 14. I am enclosing 50 Marks. Could you now buy twenty-four flowers (there must be twenty-four) in Bruhl. I am sure that the most beautiful athlete of all times will be very pleased. Thank you very much in advance!*

"*We all like and love your daughter! A few things that distinguish Stephanie: irresistibly charming, very intelligent, her natural way of behaving, dream figure, beautiful long hair. Eyes like two diamonds, etc. I could almost fill a book. For me, Stephanie is a gift from heaven to all mankind, a model in every way. There will never be anyone else like her again.*"

"*Dear Stephanie,*

"*As you can see, I am enclosing a few Marks. I really wanted to send you a present for your birthday with this letter. But I thought that was too risky. I would be very glad, my darling, if you could buy a necklace or something like that. It would then be with you in every match as a symbol of the inseparable friendship between Stephanie and her fans.*

"*The idea came to me when I heard that your personal belongings had been stolen in Brighton. My gift is therefore also meant as a consolation.*

"*I wish you all the best and above all good health on your birthday in advance, and success in your athletic career.*

"*Friends forever*"

25

It didn't matter that Parche was dangerous. On October 13, 1993, he was given two years' probation for pleading guilty to a charge of bodily injury. The verdict and sentence were a slap on the wrist for attempted murder.

Shortly after the verdict, I decided to lodge an appeal. There would be a second trial. If there had been an error, Parche would get jail time. The German courts would send a message that an attack on an international guest was unacceptable, and I'd get temporary peace of mind.

Throughout November 1993 I continued training with Bob Kersee. My body was beginning to feel fatigued, but I didn't let up. I couldn't. I was sleeping less and less since the verdict, and I needed to push harder to reach a level of total exhaustion where I was too tired to think.

I never let on to my parents that things weren't getting much easier for me. I didn't want to worry them and, looking back, I realize that I was afraid of appearing weak. On the tennis court I was always mentally tough. I could be down 4–love in a match, and I'd come back. Now, Parche had made me vulnerable. It's my fault, I thought. Why didn't I fight back? He'd stabbed me, taken away my ability to play professional tennis, and now he was making me miserable.

My father thought that I was finally on the road to recovery. He was also feeling better since his prostate surgery and, for the first time in months, he began to relax. Before we knew it, the time came for him to go back to the Mayo Clinic for his checkup. My mother flew to Rochester with him, and Zoltan and I stayed in Florida.

When the phone rang two days later, I knew from Zoltan's expression that more bad news was on the way.

"What is it, Zoltan?" I asked softly as he talked to my parents on the phone. "Let me talk to them . . . what's going on?"

He didn't hand me the phone. Instead, he finished the conversation and then hung up the receiver.

"Dad has cancer again," he told me as we sat facing each other at the kitchen table.

"The prostate cancer is back?" I asked.

"No, that's gone," he replied. "Now he has stomach cancer. They think it might have spread to one of his kidneys — if it has, they'll have to remove it."

"Okay, it's bad news, but he survived the last surgery and beat the cancer," I said. "So he'll do it again."

"Dad says that he doesn't want to go through surgery again . . . He says that whatever life he has left, that's what he'll take."

"What does that mean?" I asked.

"That he's not going to fight this time," Zoltan said quietly.

"No!" I cried. I grabbed the telephone and dialed my father's number at the Mayo Clinic. When he answered, his voice was lifeless. "Dad, you've got to fight," I said. "Our family has been through so much the last eight months. You've got to stay positive! We've been working hard together to get my game back on track — I can't do it without you. I need you here to help me make my comeback. I need you to help me put the attack behind me!"

My father finally agreed to go in for the surgery. I was scared when I hung up the phone. He didn't sound like the man I'd known all my life. Instead, he sounded weak and tired. I wanted to fly up to Rochester, but Dad insisted that I stay in Sarasota and continue working with Bob Kersee. Zoltan flew up to the Mayo Clinic, and I began training twice as hard as before. I didn't want to be home, didn't want to think about my father in the hospital, or Parche wandering free.

Ten days later my father came home. He was so white and thin that

I was afraid to hug him. When he showed me his scar, I was appalled. It went clear from one side of his body to the other — as if he'd been gutted. The surgery had been a success: they'd taken out an enormous tumor and found no trace of cancer in his kidneys. But this time, my father's recovery was even slower than before.

It's so hard to watch a parent suffer. If I could have taken away the pain, I would have. Our family had been through hell the last year. The cancer was the last thing any of us needed. Still, it reminded me of what was important. I would have gladly given up tennis if it had meant my father would remain healthy. As it turned out, I think my comeback was one of the things he clung to when he'd all but given up hope. The fact that I needed him — as a coach and as a father — while I dealt with the trauma of the attack, made him fight harder to beat the cancer.

In early December Bob Kersee and Jackie returned home for the holidays and I decided to take a week off training. My journey from the attack back to the court was about to take a twist which would break me completely before I could ever become whole again.

$$\left(26\right)$$

In early December 1993 the dreams began again. Most nights I dreamt that I was back in Hamburg. I stepped out onto the court and began to play. Each time I looked into the stands, there was Parche's face. I called over to the umpire, "Please make that man leave, he hurt me!" The umpire turned to look at the man. When he turned back, it was Parche's face in the chair — Parche smiling at me in the Arthur Ashe baseball cap he was wearing the day he watched my practice. The day before he stabbed me.

I ran over to my parents' box and asked them to make him go away — to protect me — but their seats were empty. And then the lightning pain in my back. I fell onto the court, and looked up into Parche's leering face. I tried to scream, but this time no sound came out of my mouth.

I turned my head to see that my opponent was about to serve. "I've been stabbed, stop the match," I sobbed. My voice sounded strained and small. The ball was served.

The umpire announced, "Point Maleeva," and then added, "Ms. Seles, if you do not return to play you will receive a warning."

"I can't return to play, I've been stabbed! Why hasn't anyone noticed?" There was a lump in my throat and my words came out in hoarse croaks. And then I looked back up at Parche, and he was raising his arms to strike again. I could see the curved blade as it caught the afternoon sun, and felt the air part as it sliced toward my body. And then I screamed and screamed and screamed . . .

"Monica, it's a dream, wake up," my mother said as she shook me.

"Please, wake up!" Night after night, the same thing. Screaming in my sleep, waking in a cold sweat with my mother standing over me, looking frightened and worried. As the scream reverberated in my mind, I told her I was all right. I asked her to sleep in my bed for the night, to hold me in her arms like a baby.

There was a lot to be thankful for: my father was recovering from his second bout of cancer; I'd turned twenty on December 2 — a birthday I might never have seen; my family was together at Christmas; and physically I was still in the best shape I'd ever been, despite my decision to take time off training. Moreover, the appeal of the Parche case had been lodged in the German courts. He would be tried again.

So why was I feeling emotionally troubled? Time. I'd had too much of it since the Kersees left Sarasota. Taking a week off training had been a bad idea, so I tried to begin again. But I couldn't make myself exercise. Just get on the treadmill and walk, I thought with growing concern. But a few minutes after I'd started, I'd step off. Working out had been my weapon against the depression and fears that lingered from the attack. There were still places to fly, to drive, but exhaustion filled my bones with lead and made me too tired to go anywhere.

At the end of December we went to Vail for four days so that Dr. Hawkins could check my shoulder. I was hoping to get fit and resume training, hoping that the exhaustion from exercise would help me fight my demons.

I returned home and the situation got worse. I began to have rages. I'd storm out of a room and sit in the quiet stillness of my bedroom until the anger passed. Then I'd pretend that nothing had happened.

I began to reread the police transcripts of Parche's arrest, memorizing the letters he wrote to another athlete whose careless words had angered him, and those he wrote to Steffi and her mother. Parche was clearly a threat, and no matter how many times I read his statements, evaluations, and letters, I couldn't understand why he had hurt me, and why he'd gone free.

How could Parche have hated another human being enough to stab her in the back? I wondered over and over again. My mind circled the attack, the questions, the fears, visiting each moment and then going for more, gulping at every word and detail like desperately needed oxygen, and then keeping that air inside until it was stale . . . until it was poison.

I began to sit in the den of my home for hours at a time, not watching television, or listening to music, but sitting in silence and thinking about the attack.

"Monica, go outside and get some fresh air," my mother would suggest.

"I will in a little while," I'd reply with a smile.

After Vail, the crying began again. Initially, I hadn't been able to hide my tears from my family; this time, when a wave of emotions came over me I'd pinch myself hard. Usually the pain stopped the tears, but if it didn't, I'd make some excuse to leave the room. Then I'd go into my bathroom, shut the door and sink onto the white marble floor. I'd sit there, arms wrapped tightly around my legs, and sob. Eventually I would wash my face with cold water and leave the bathroom, eyes clear, a smile on my face. I thought I was fooling everyone, but I was only fooling myself.

I couldn't stand strangers, unknown faces, well-meaning fans who gave me sympathy and reduced me to tears. I refused all interviews, and closed the blinds in my house. I began to wear dark, baggy clothes.

"Monica Seles will return to professional tennis for the 1994 Australian Open." That's what the headlines read in early January. They were representative of many untrue rumors about my comeback that somehow made it to print. I'd never said that I was going to play the Australian.

"Stephanie, this has got to stop," I told my manager on the phone on January 5. "All these false reports are making me look like an idiot, because everyone thinks I'm pulling out of tournaments." IMG sent out a press release on the morning of January 6 that I wasn't playing the Australian.

That day was tough for me. I wandered around my house, going from room to room. Finally, I switched on the television in the den and caught a special news report — skater Nancy Kerrigan had been attacked at an ice-skating rink during the Olympic trials. I watched in dread as the cameras showed Nancy lying on the floor behind the rink, holding her knee. She was sobbing as her father picked her up and carried her away for medical attention. I recognized the shocked and confused look on her face.

It had happened again. That's all I could think as I watched the news. Another athlete has been violently attacked in her own arena. At that point, no one knew that the attack, which involved striking Nancy on the knee with a metal bar, was motivated by the greed of a fellow skater and her husband.

Up until the Kerrigan attack, it seemed as if no one took my stabbing seriously. Now it had happened again. Two athletes had been attacked

— not because of their personalities, but because of their talent, drive and determination. Maybe now the sports world will do something to protect us, I thought. Neither of us had been killed, but perhaps the fact that the same type of crime had been committed again would catch the attention of the media and our respective organizations.

That afternoon Stephanie called me to ask for a statement on the Kerrigan attack. I told her to release one saying that my thoughts were with Nancy and I hoped they'd catch whoever had done such a senseless and savage thing. We released the statement that night.

"Monica Seles has been frightened away from her comeback at the Australian Open because of the Kerrigan attack." That's what the headlines read the following morning, regardless of the fact that I'd released my statement about Australia hours before I knew anything about Nancy's attack; regardless of the fact that I wouldn't have played the Open anyway.

I stopped reading the newspaper or watching the television. I'd sleep for a few hours during the middle of the day, then shuffle into the den in the same baggy clothes I'd worn all week. I'd sink onto my couch and stare at the white marble floor. I no longer tried to hide my feelings from my parents, who watched with growing fear as I slid into an abyss of depression. When they tried to pull me out, I'd begin to sob until they couldn't bear it any longer and they'd drop the issue.

When I wasn't lying on my couch, I was in the kitchen searching for food. It didn't matter *what* I ate, only that I ate. I'd bring bags of chips into the den and consume them. I'd take large rectangular cartons of ice cream and scoop the coldness into my mouth until the container was empty. I didn't even know what flavors I ate, only that the physical act of eating felt good.

"Monica, this isn't right," my mother said repeatedly. "You're eating uncontrollably. You eat and eat, and you can't be that hungry because you're not getting any exercise. You're gaining a lot of weight and you look pale and unhealthy."

I kept eating. Food was something that no one could take away from me. When my mother stopped buying ice cream and junk food, I began to make 5:00 am food runs. The grocery store was empty then, and I could shop without being noticed. By the end of February I'd gone from 140 pounds to about 175 pounds.

Throughout February I hid inside my home. Sometimes I'd take calls from Stephanie or from Betsy Nagelsen; sometimes I'd sit and reread transcripts from the German police; sometimes I'd just cry for hours. The only constants in my life were food, fear, and depression. At the age of twenty, I felt as if my life was over. Is this what it's going to be like? I asked myself. No personal or professional life?

The press, however, remained interested in my life, regardless of the fact that I was no longer playing tennis, regardless of the fact that what they now wrote had nothing to do with my public personality, but intruded on my private domain.

(28)

I granted no interviews in the winter of 1994. Since the media couldn't talk to me, they wrote about the only thing available: my house — a house they photographed from helicopters that hovered over my backyard, noisy machines that broke my father's pain-filled sleep as he recovered from his cancer operations, and added to my own fearful delusions. And from my home, they drew their own conclusions about me, my family, and my life.

My house in Florida was completed in June 1992. One of the things I required was a six-foot wall around the property. I spend a large percentage of my time in the public eye, and I wanted some privacy. Many other top players, including Steffi Graf, have walls around their properties. If I didn't have a gated home, fans would walk right up to my front door. While most wouldn't mean any harm, I have a right to peace and quiet with my family and friends. In addition, for the first time I was going to have a tennis court in my backyard. I wanted to practice in privacy.

After the attack the press laid into my house: all of a sudden the walls were ten feet high, and there were cameras, alarms and gates everywhere. I think the media were frustrated by my silence and wanted to provoke me into talking. But the truth is that the house was designed and built before April 1993. We didn't change anything after the attack.

We moved into our new home in July of '92. We'd been in Europe during most of the construction, and hadn't had much time to design the interior of the house. I picked a French colonial style with high ceilings and long windows. Because we weren't there, the builder had to make some decisions about the kitchen design and appliances, even the floorplan of our bedrooms.

However, one very specific detail was my idea: I wanted swan fixtures on all my drawers, faucets and hooks. There was something about the gracefully curved swans that reminded me of fairy tales. As a child, I loved the story of the ugly duckling who turned into the snow-white swan. The swan fixtures also reminded me of my grandmother. In Yugoslavia she lived close to a pond and she'd take me for walks to see the swans. We'd sit on a bench and feed them breadcrumbs.

The problem with my swans was that each one was hand-crafted and expensive. We were so over budget on the house that I couldn't rationalize the cost. The builder solved that problem by finding chrome swans instead of the more expensive brass ones. I ordered the swans, but still flinched at the price. Everyone says that when you build a house, the cost always exceeds your estimate. Next time, I'll buy a model home. I'll probably still want fairy-tale fixtures, though.

The house I built was just a house — not the fortress that the media dreamt up. They drew upon what they knew about the house — how much it cost, how big it was, its structure and design, to conclude that it was indeed a castle. I was a princess behind its walls, rarely, if ever, exposed to harm or evil.

"Monica Seles needs to grow up and learn that life isn't a fairy tale," a reporter wrote after I was stabbed in Hamburg. He said that the reason I was so emotionally devastated by the attack was that I'd never seen tough times; I didn't understand what reality was.

My first thought after reading the article was that the attack hadn't been a part of anyone's reality. If you sell drugs on the corner, or rob a bank, or mug someone, maybe then a knife in the back is a reality. In life there are countless random acts of violence — but on a tennis court? It was something that had never happened before. If I'd known that being attacked while I rested between changeovers was part of the deal, I would never have become a tennis player.

And what did that reporter know about my life, anyway? Did he understand what it was like to live in a socialist country, where only a connection with someone important made it possible to book a tennis court, or obtain a visa? Did he have a grandfather who was in a prison camp because he was willing to fight for his beliefs, and ultimately to die for them? A grandmother who was a devout Catholic in a country that forbade religion? I did. And I understood these things when I was eight.

Did that reporter know how it felt to leave Yugoslavia and my family at twelve and try to survive in a place where I didn't understand the language or the people? To leave my home with no guarantee that I was doing the right thing? To take my parents away from their friends and relatives, from their livelihoods, knowing that the family finances now rested on my twelve-year-old shoulders? Had that reporter ever heard the words, "Monica, don't panic, but they found another cancer and I have to go into surgery tomorrow." Had he ever felt a slice of burning agony bolt down his back and turned to see his attacker raise both arms to strike again?

29

One exciting thing happened in March of 1994: my mother and I became American citizens.

We'd been waiting for five years and we were thrilled when the call came that we had both been accepted to receive our US citizenships, provided we passed the citizenship exam. It was enough to lift my depression momentarily.

"We've got to study," my mom said anxiously. There was a list of 100 questions from which the citizenship board would randomly test us. A few weeks after we'd been notified, we were called to the immigration office in Miami for our tests. Our whole family drove down. Coincidentally, the Lipton tournament was going on when we arrived there.

I was filled with apprehension. The immigration people were considerate of my situation, and to my surprise they gave us a private room for our test. When I'd answered all my questions correctly, the interviewer said, "I have just one more for you. Who was the youngest president of the United States?"

"That wasn't on the list," I replied.

"Did you memorize all 100 questions?" she asked, amazed.

"I guess so," I said.

"Answer the question anyway," the woman instructed.

It was between Clinton and Kennedy. "Kennedy?" I asked. The woman nodded. I'd answered that one correctly, too. My mother also passed her exam with flying colors. We went into another room and made our pledge of allegiance to the United States. Then we received beautiful certificates and had our pictures taken for our American passports. I'd felt like an American citizen for years, but now I truly was one.

30

Some gifts can be held in the palm of your hand — a US passport, a golden trophy or a crystal bowl; others aren't so tangible, but are no less valuable. On the contrary, sometimes they're worth more than anything else in the world. A father's love is one of those invisible, invaluable things.

"Monica, I have to talk to you," my father said after we returned from Miami. I looked up blankly from my couch, staring through the darkness that surrounded me like a woolen blanket.

"Monica, things cannot go on this way. It's so hard for me, as a father, to see you like this."

"Dad, I don't want to talk," I said abruptly, as I had each time he had tried to talk seriously to me.

"Forget about tennis," my dad continued, "Let's just concentrate on you. You're destroying your health by overeating and not exercising, destroying your life by hiding in this house. Monica, you're letting one person take everything away from you — that's not right! There have been a lot of tough times over the last year, but you can get through them. You're strong, Monica."

Am I? I wondered. I looked at my father's pained face and began to cry. "I can't," I said. "Every day I tell myself to get a grip, but then it hits me — my God, everything is so crappy . . ." I got up and moved toward my bathroom door, seeking the one place where I could cry for hours without feeling guilty for my weakness.

"Monica, sit down," my dad said. "I know that you want to run, but we've got to face this."

I ran anyway and slammed my bathroom door closed behind me.

Dad followed and knocked. "Monica, you can't run from your problems. It's so hard for me to upset you, but no matter what any of the family does, it doesn't change the fact that you're miserable and getting worse every day. Please come out."

Slowly I opened the door. I was crying so hard that I couldn't catch my breath.

"You can't escape your problems by crying," my dad continued. "And I can't seem to help you, so you've got to go back and see Dr. May. It doesn't mean you're weak, Monica. There's nothing to be ashamed of. It's just something you have to do. I'll give you two weeks to make the arrangements. If you don't, I'm going to drive you to the airport and put you on the plane."

"I don't deserve this," I sobbed. I was living in a prison of fear. Parche had stolen my life, tennis career and income (I only had one company who sponsored me during the two years I was out of the game). That evening I promised my dad I'd go back to Lake Tahoe and see Dr. May. I don't know if I said the words to soften the look of worry etched across his face, or because I wanted to believe there was a chance for help. I think it was a little of both. However, when it came to taking action I couldn't cope.

My father saw that I was not making plans to fly to California. He came into my room a week after our conversation and said, "Get some things together and drive to the airport with Zoltan. He's taking you to see Dr. May."

I knew that arguing with my dad wouldn't work, and that if I promised to make arrangements, he wouldn't believe me. So I packed my bags and Zoltan and I flew to California.

This time, it was different. The first time I'd seen Dr. May I'd been in denial, certain that if I wished hard enough, trained long enough, flew far enough, the attack would disappear. In March 1994 I had come to realize that there was no escape. And knowing I was trapped made it easier to accept help.

I spent two weeks in Tahoe going to therapy. At first I just cried, but slowly I began to open up to Dr. May, slowly I began to trust him. We started to talk about the last three months and how I'd succumbed to my depression and fears until they controlled me.

"Monica," he said after I'd spoken for hours, "you're only twenty years old, and you're alive but you're not living." I felt a lump growing in my throat. He was right. I'd been going through some of the motions, but I hadn't been living my life for almost a year.

"What do you see yourself doing, ideally, that would make you happy?" Dr. May asked one afternoon.

I hadn't thought in terms of happiness for a long time and it took me a while to answer. "I guess playing tennis is what makes me really happy. Tennis has always been my world, and all of a sudden I'm out of it."

"Do you see yourself playing for fun, or going back to competition?"

"I cannot imagine sitting in a chair during the changeover of a match," I said quickly. "But, if I could recover enough to maybe practice again on the court in my backyard, and play where nobody could watch me, I would be happy."

"What else would make you happy?" he went on.

"To have a normal life again," I said softly. "To be able to talk to people and not start crying . . ."

"You can have those things," he began. "But you're an athlete, and you know that tough goals aren't reached easily. To attain them, you're going to have to deal with a lot of emotions. There will be days when you feel worse than you do right now, because I'm going to ask you some tough questions that you're not going to want to answer — like what it felt like to be violated by another human being, the nightmares you have, and how Parche's face looked after he stabbed you. I'm going to want you to talk about your irrational fears, and I'm going to push you to beat them. And I know that you can beat them."

Dr. May and I talked about my depression and he explained that I

127

was experiencing post-traumatic stress disorder. All the shock, fear, depression and anxiety I'd tried to run away from had finally come to the surface. There were moments when I'd cry, and Dr. May would tell me that it was okay to feel the way I felt. To hear someone say that what I was going through was understandable, even normal, meant a lot to me.

My life had lost its balance, and Dr. May was there to help me to regain it. We worked through a model called the "ABCs of psychology." "A" stands for affect, and that's feelings and sensations; "B" is for behaviors; and "C" stands for cognitions, which are thoughts and dreams. Dr. May explained that when my feelings, behaviors and cognitions became balanced, I'd be able to control my depression.

Together, we began to set some short-term goals. Dr. May told me that one of my first goals should be to get out in the fresh air. Activity, he said, was a distractor — a way to control my fears and anxieties. When I returned to Florida, he suggested I should walk around my yard each day. For a start, Dr. May and I went hiking in the mountains. I couldn't keep up. I was in such bad shape that I was breathing hard and had to ask him to slow down. The hike really showed me how far I'd deteriorated since the fall of 1993.

"Monica, I want you to try to be around people. You need slowly to bring a sense of balance back to your life," Dr. May explained as we hiked. My stomach flipped at the thought. Hiking in the solitude of the mountains was one thing; being around people was another. By the time my ten days of therapy ended, I was emotionally drained. Still, I was afraid to go home — afraid I wouldn't have the strength to return for more therapy.

"There's no way we can do nonstop therapy," Dr. May explained. "Even though I'd like to keep you out here for the next three months, you need to go home. Take some time to work on your first set of goals. But I want you back here in five weeks, and I'm going to write your next session in my appointment book. For the time being, we'll work through ten days of therapy, several hours each day, with time off between."

I watched as he wrote my appointment down. Seeing my name on the page, knowing that he expected me to return, gave me hope that I'd be able to make the trip.

When I got back home there was a message from Betsy Nagelsen. She'd just returned from a tournament, and she invited me to her home in Orlando. "Just come down and spend some time with my brother and me," Betsy suggested. My mom and I drove down a few days later.

While I was in Orlando, I began to open up to Betsy and tell her of my fears and difficulties. As always, she listened and offered advice. "Whatever you need to do, I'm here for you," she said. Then, with a grin, she enticed me out to try waterskiing. We spent the afternoon in the water, and there were even a few moments when I forgot my problems and let myself bask in Betsy's warmth and spirit.

When I returned to Sarasota, I walked into my backyard and stared at the tennis court, at every line, every angle. I walked to one corner, and sat down in the grass. I thought about all the good things that tennis had brought me — all the tournaments and Grand Slams I'd won, the tough matches where I'd been down and fought back.

Then I thought about how tennis had given me so much, and then taken it all away. I felt depression creep through the grass and sit down beside me. Slowly, I stood and walked back inside the house to reread my police transcripts and eat a carton of ice cream.

During the weeks before my return to Dr. May, I thought about all the things we had discussed and tried to put his suggestions into action. With my family's help I found ways to distract myself from the fear and depression that gripped me. I began to walk around my backyard with my parents. I didn't stay outside long, but at least I was out. At the end of the first week in Florida I decided to ride my bike down our quiet street with my mother. It felt good to be outside the walls of my home. Later, Mom and I visited a neighbor. I still wasn't sleeping at night, and my eating was out of control. Small goals, I reminded myself when I was overwhelmed by how far I had to go. Small goals.

31

I'd given my word to Dr. May that I'd return to Tahoe, and anyone who knows me knows that I hate to go back on my word. At the beginning of May Zoltan and I flew back out to California. We stayed in the same hotel, in the same room on the top floor of the building. I was still afraid to be alone, and Zoltan took care of me as only a big brother knows how.

When I saw Dr. May again I realized that I was starting to like him as a person. He's young in spirit, married with three kids, and could relate to me on a comfortable level. In addition, he'd worked with Olympic athletes and with people who'd been through situations similar to my own. I was surprised to find that I trusted him.

We started to talk about the actual attack. It was the first time I'd described the details that haunted me — the bloody shirt, the knife, Parche's face. I told Dr. May about my nightmares. We even talked about one of my biggest worries — that I couldn't visualize myself walking out on a court ever again: when I tried to imagine it, all I saw was darkness.

We began to work on techniques to control my nightmares and negative thoughts. The first step was to become aware. The second was a conditioning technique called the "Stop, Think, Technique." The basic principle was to reward my mind for cutting off negative thoughts by replacing them with positive ones. For example, when I woke up from a bad dream, I said the word "stop" to cut off the action and wake fully from the nightmare. Then I said "focus" to draw upon a positive memory to replace the negative thoughts. I didn't use the technique only for nightmares; when I was overwhelmed by exaggerated fears and anxiety, I used the same device.

At first "focus" was difficult for me. It took me almost a month to find one good thought that was strong enough to replace the bad ones. Finally, the thought that I was only twenty and still had a chance of a normal life was powerful enough to overcome some of the dreams and fears. Ultimately, the technique worked like a filter. It funneled out the bad images and left good ones.

The nightmares were upsetting, but they weren't the biggest issue. One of the hardest things for me to understand was the fact that I took the attack very personally. Dr. May explained that I had to let it go, comprehend that what Parche did was out of my hands. That would take some time. In the meantime, we worked on a third technique.

The relaxation technique Dr. May taught me was called "systematic desensitization," which focused on tightening and then releasing sixteen major muscle groups. I'd clench and unclench each muscle until it felt loose and warm. When I concentrated on my muscles, it switched the focus from my brain to my body and I forgot my fears.

It took a while before I was able to relax completely. When I'd learned the technique, Dr. May began to explain how we'd use it to help me. "Now that you know how to relax," he said, "we'll begin to imagine situations that make you uncomfortable, and eventually we'll move to ones that make you fearful, like the attack. Ultimately, your relaxation and fears will reciprocally inhibit each other and the fear will go away."

"Lie on the floor, close your eyes, and go through each of your muscle groups," he suggested during one of our sessions. Fifteen minutes later I felt relaxed. "Now imagine yourself walking in a public place. Try to feel comfortable with the people around you as you walk. See yourself saying hello to them." I felt my heart begin to race. I focused on clenching my muscles again. Slowly the technique began to work. The next week Dr. May introduced uncomfortable situations into my mind when I was relaxed, and I tried to learn how to feel comfortable with them.

"Can you see yourself walking onto a tennis court yet?" he asked one day.

"That I cannot see," I replied sadly. It would take another year before I was able to see myself playing professional tennis again.

When our session was up, Zoltan arrived to drive me back to the hotel.

"Don't be discouraged," Dr. May said when I left his office. I tried to smile. "Hey, Zoltan, try to get your sister to go to a public place on your way to the hotel," he suggested to my brother.

On the way back to the hotel, we drove by a little coffee shop. "Want to stop for some coffee?" Zoltan asked. Because it was Zoltan, because with my brother I felt safe, I said yes. It was a beautiful day and we sat on the deck of the shop and drank our coffee. It felt so good to be doing something normal. Nothing bad happened.

A week later I went into a supermarket with Zoltan. We walked down the aisles and I constantly looked over my shoulder. There were so many people behind me. "Stay calm, Monica," I said under my breath. "Just buy what you need and get out." The supermarket was a hard one, but the next time it got a little better. I'd accomplished two more goals.

32

"I have to ask this question sooner or later," Dr. May said. "How about going out on the tennis court and hitting for a few minutes?"

"I can't," I said sadly.

"Why not?"

"If I step onto a court, that means that I'll have to return to competitive tennis," I reasoned. "And I can never do that because I can't sit on the court with the stands to my back."

"Monica, I'm just talking about hitting a couple of balls at my club," he pressed.

"There will be too many people watching," I replied.

"You can hit early in the morning when no one is out there."

"Maybe in a few days . . ." I said to get off the subject.

"Tell me what you're thinking."

"I'm thinking about the net, and the chairs set up for breaks during competitive tournaments. And when I see those chairs in my mind, the attack comes back," I replied softly.

"That's a normal feeling, but you've got to replace it with something positive. I'll bring my wife and you can hit with Zoltan — it'll feel really comfortable," Dr. May continued.

"I didn't bring my racket," I hedged.

"Zoltan told me that you've brought your racket to Tahoe every visit. He said you even brought it the first time you came out in March," he replied. It was true. For some reason I'd always brought my racket on the plane to California. "You want to play. Five minutes, Monica. Five

minutes on the court won't hurt you. Pick the time, day or night —
just call me and we'll be there."

"Do you really think early morning is the quietest time?" I asked.

"Yes — we're at 6,000 feet and it's chilly in the morning. No one
wants to play until it warms up," he explained. "How about tomorrow?"

"Okay," I said nervously. "Okay."

I must have stretched on the grass beside the court for at least a half
hour. Finally Zoltan said, "Monica, just try it. You won't know until
you do." I picked up my racket and walked to one side of the court.
Zoltan stood on the other side, waiting for me to hit him a ball. And
then we were hitting. Not just rallying, but playing good tennis.

I lost myself for half an hour — there was just the ball, my racket
and the player on the other side. I felt the familiar rhythm of the game,
the vibration down my arm when the ball made contact with my strings.
Then I rested for a moment to catch my breath and all the fears flooded
back. "I've had enough," I said nervously, and ran to the grass.

"I can't do this," I told Dr. May when he came over to me. "It's not
possible to do this!"

"Monica, that was a great effort. Think positive thoughts," he said.
"You just played tennis for a half hour. Next time, maybe you'll play
for forty minutes. The time after that, an hour. Remember, small goals,
small steps."

I returned to Florida. Every couple of days I'd go out on the court
in my backyard. Sometimes I'd hit for a few minutes with my brother,
sometimes I'd just walk on and off. When Betsy Nagelsen called to invite
me back down to Orlando I was relieved. I needed a break from my
goals.

Betsy and I did a lot of talking during my visits. Sometimes her
brother, Jimmy, would join us. Our conversations helped me to get
some perspective on the attack and my life. Betsy spent countless hours
telling me not what to do, but how she looked at life; how she accepted
that some things were out of her control. "There are bad people out

there," she said, "you know that. And some of them are going to try to take a shot at you — it happens to everyone. Tennis is nothing. It's what you do. But how you choose to live your life, how you choose to find peace, that's what's important."

Those conversations were vital. Dr. May was giving me a practical way to deal with my depression and emotions, but Betsy filled in another part of the puzzle. She was the friend and sounding board I needed. She also gave me another gift: she helped me to find joy in tennis again.

"Hey, Monica, would you mind hitting a few balls with me?" Betsy asked as we walked up the dock from her boat. "I'm trying to get ready for a doubles tournament, and I could use the practice."

"I haven't played much," I said nervously. "I wouldn't give you a good workout."

"Come on," she wheedled as we walked toward her tennis court. "Just stand in one corner — you don't even have to move — and hit me balls."

It's hard to say no to Betsy. I took a racket and walked onto her court. We played for the next hour, and I found myself laughing as Betsy alternated between practicing and joking around. "Can you take it easy on me?" she said at one point. I'd been so focused on giving her a good practice that I'd begun to hit really hard shots. After so many months off the court, my eye–hand coordination was still right on. When we were done, Betsy dropped her racket on the court and said, "Monica, I just want to tell you that if you don't return to competitive tennis, it'll be too bad because your talent is unbelievable."

A few weeks later I played my first match. It was in Betsy's backyard. Her husband, Mark McCormack, and I teamed up in a doubles match against Betsy and my father. Mark, Betsy and I are competitive by nature. My father, on the other hand, doesn't care. For him the joy is in playing well and having fun, not winning. That day he was happy to be out in the sunshine with friends. Most of all, he was thrilled to see me smiling on a tennis court.

Everyone on the court had his or her own agenda. I was trying to play each shot perfectly — not too hard to my dad, angled right for Betsy. Don't get me wrong, I wanted to win — some things never change. Betsy and Mark also wanted to win. Unfortunately, Betsy was partnered with Dad, who was laughing and joking around the entire time. It was still close, but in the end Mark and I took the match.

It wasn't a Grand Slam win, but it felt really good. That afternoon I wandered around Betsy's home and let some favorite memories float to the surface. One of them was the 1992 Australian Open.

(33)

The Australian Open has always been one of my favorites. First, because of the koala bears. I love visiting them at the Melbourne Zoo — even though they sleep most of the day. Second, because the Australian Open is the most convenient of all the Grand Slams. I can bike from our rented house to the stadium, and all the restaurants and stores are close. Convenience isn't so important when you're vacationing, but it is when you're playing a tournament, and when you know you'll be playing throughout Europe and staying in hotels for the next two months.

The third reason I like playing the Australian is that it's the quietest Grand Slam. It's easy to get practice courts. And Australian spectators are the calmest, most supportive crowd in tennis. Since the Australian Open is the first major tournament of the season, it's nice to begin quietly. The fourth reason is that the stadium can be converted from outdoor to indoor in a matter of minutes. If rain sets in, there is a motorized cover for the arena that allows players to continue their matches. Since rain delays can stall a player's momentum, even make her lose a match, the cover is really important.

The 1992 Australian Open was one of the easier Grand Slams for me. I made it to the finals without difficulty, beating Anke Huber in the quarters and Aranxta Sanchez Vicario in the semis. Then I faced Mary Joe Fernandez, whom I'd beaten in a scorching drawn-out semifinal at the '91 Australian Open. I knew Mary Joe wanted to erase the memory of that match with a big win. I would have felt the same. My only goal for the '92 finals was to keep it short. I didn't want to be dragged into a long, three-set match. Mary Joe is a steady back-court player so, if I didn't hit winners, each point would take forever.

I stepped onto center court in the midday heat. This time I closed out Mary Joe in an uneventful match, 6–2, 6–3. I'd won my second Australian Grand Slam. It was a great way to begin my '92 season.

My next major tournament was in May, in Barcelona. It was a new tournament for me. Every season there are a certain number of matches I have to play, and a few new ones I can add to my list. That year I added Barcelona because I'd never been there before. The city was beautiful, but the tournament turned out to be a tough one.

I played Arantxa Sanchez Vicario in the finals. Arantxa has a wicked backhand and the ability to retrieve the most ungettable shots. She's strong, fast, and also a native of Barcelona. Our match took place only months before the 1992 Barcelona Olympics. Arantxa was determined to win in her own backyard.

The spectators were fair. They cheered for me when I walked out onto the court, clapped when I hit winners. But there was overwhelming support for Arantxa in the stadium. This was her hometown; in a few months she'd represent her country in the Olympics. Everyone, with the exception of me, wanted her to win the tournament.

The match was on very slow red clay. That made it even easier for Arantxa to run down every single ball. I had to work twice as hard for each point. She won the first set, 3–6. I took the second, 6–2. By the third, I could no longer feel my legs. I'd run so far they were numb. I took the third set, 6–3, to win the match. I should have been elated, but I don't remember feeling anything but relief. I walked off the court covered in red clay, sweat running down my back and exhaustion weighing heavily on my shoulders.

The next day I left for the Italian Open in Rome. The tournament was uneventful until the finals. I lost the match to Gabriela Sabatini. Gaby just outplayed me that day and took the Open in two sets. "Good match, Gaby," I said as we shook hands at the net.

I don't like losing, but if I have to lose to anyone, Gaby would probably be one of my first choices: she's consistently nice — win or lose. I think her family is very like my own. Her parents sit quietly in their box during matches. They cheer for both players and never try to distract their daughter's opponent — not like some parents and coaches. They appreciate good tennis, whether or not their daughter wins. I lost the Italian Open, but at least I lost to a great lady.

After the Italian I was feeling tired. One of the toughest things for players who live in the United States is the length of the European season. By the time I return home after Wimbledon, I've been in Europe for three months — three months in hotels, living out of suitcases, sleeping in different beds. After the Italian Open, all I wanted to do was go home. But I still had the French Open and Wimbledon.

There are approximately two weeks between the Italian and the French Opens. I decided to stay in Rome to prepare. During that time I did several taped television interviews for the media so they'd have footage to run for the French Open. At the time, I was a blonde; and I went to Paris as a blonde. But when I began the French Open, I was raven haired and some of the press were somewhat upset.

I didn't think. That's the bottom line. When I arrived in Paris a friend arranged for me to have my hair cut. She said I'd look good as a brunette. Since that's my natural color, it seemed like a good idea. I went to the famous salon she'd suggested. I was supposed to have an appointment, but when I arrived they didn't have me penciled in. However, someone recognized me, so the stylist agreed to cut and color my hair anyway.

"You'd look great with jet-black hair," the stylist suggested.

"Sure, why not?" I said with a laugh. "It's just hair color — if I don't like it, I can always change it back."

Several hours later I faced a young woman I hardly recognized. My hair was as black as night, and the stylist had put bright red lipstick on me. It was a dramatic look — I loved it. When I saw my friend that night, she was pleasantly shocked. As it turned out, I'd gone to the wrong salon and that was why I hadn't had an appointment. No harm done, I thought.

I was wrong. When I walked into the locker room before my first-round match, Arantxa Sanchez Vicario didn't even recognize me. She walked straight past without looking twice. And after the match the media went crazy. All the TV interviews I'd previously done were worthless. They couldn't use footage of me as a blonde when I now had black hair — it wouldn't make sense to the viewers, they said angrily. What could I do? I apologized and repeated as many interviews as possible.

It wasn't the end of the world: I even had some fun doing the interviews again. But I didn't need the distraction. This was my third French Open, and I wanted to focus on defending my title. The last woman to win three consecutive French singles titles was Hilde Sperling in 1935–7. In June 1992 I had the chance to match Hilde's accomplishment, and I wanted that third title. As it turned out, I'd have to fight harder than I'd ever fought before, just to get to the finals. It would be the toughest Grand Slam of my life in terms of sheer stamina.

I almost went out in the fourth round. Akiko Kijimuta of Japan, ranked 150th, had me 1–4 in the third set, with one set apiece. She ran down everything I hit and sent the balls back, low and hard, her knees touching the ground. She rifled winners from every corner of the court. I couldn't hit anything, but I was determined not to go out in the fourth round after winning the French Open the past two years. I fought back in the cold and rain and won the next five games to take the third set, 6–4. I'd been lucky, but the match left me tired and I needed some distraction.

I went shopping. I've never been an extravagant person. If you don't have money, and then you get some, you go one of two ways. I'm a saver, not a spender. Still, I've always loved high fashion. When I was a kid in Yugoslavia, there was a wooden newspaper stand across from our apartment that sold fashion magazines. The woman who ran it used to loan them to me — *Vogue, Cosmo, Elle*. I'd take them to my bedroom and pore over the pictures of Armani, Versace, and Chanel dresses —

especially Chanel. So it wasn't surprising that I found myself in the Chanel boutique in Paris.

No one came up to me. I was an eighteen-year-old in jeans and sneakers, and I wandered through the store being noticed, but not helped. Finally, a saleswoman recognized me and asked if I'd like to try on one of the dresses. Would I? I spent the next few hours trying on dresses, suits, scarves, and headbands. I fell in love with a bright green Chanel suit. I remember fingering the classic gold buttons and looking in the mirror. The suit was far too sophisticated for an eighteen-year-old, but I didn't care.

"Would you like to try on the matching headband?" the saleswoman asked.

I pulled the flowered band through my hair. "If I win my next round, I'm going to bring my mom here to see this suit," I explained to the woman. "If she likes it, maybe I'll buy it." I beat Jennifer Capriati in the quarterfinals (6–2, 6–2) and returned to the boutique with my mother the next day.

"Monica, it's beautiful," my mom began, "but you could buy a small car for the same price; maybe a used one for the price of the headband alone!"

"I know," I said ruefully. "Let's just see how my semifinal match goes. The suit is too much, but if I win the semis, maybe I'll buy the headband." Whenever I play a tournament, I try to buy myself something to remind me of the place, and that gives me a challenge to play well.

I played Gabriela Sabatini in the semifinals of the French Open. I was down in the first set, 2–4, and really dragging. I can't finish this match, I thought in exhaustion. I tried to move slowly between points so that I could catch my breath. I even took chances to rest by tying and retying my shoelaces. The freezing weather and rain were sapping my strength — the cold I'd developed and antibiotics I was taking made matters worse. The colder I got, the more weary I became. The clay was slow, and the balls very heavy.

I can't go on, I realized with growing panic. Then I dug deep and somehow found the strength. Come on, Monica, go for it, I told myself. In the post-match press interview Gaby would tell the media, "[Monica] seemed tired and then suddenly she started hitting the ball very hard. I don't know where she got the power." I came back and took the first set, 6–3. Gaby won the second, 4–6, but with visions of that green flowered band, I closed the third, 6–4.

The next morning I went to the Chanel salon and bought that headband. I fingered the suit longingly, but didn't buy it. "Maybe if I win tomorrow," I told my mom with a little smile. Then I went home and crawled into bed. It was the first time I hadn't practiced before a final: a risky decision, but I was worried I wouldn't be able to play in the finals if I didn't rest. I'd need all my strength to face Steffi Graf the following day.

I knew it would be a difficult finals match even before I saw the look of determination on Steffi's face as we stepped onto center court. I'd taken the French Grand Slam title from Steffi in '90, and she wanted to take it back. I was determined not to let her: I wanted to win my third French Open. If I won, maybe it would give me the push I needed to buy that Chanel suit.

I took the first set, 6–2. Steffi fought back and took the next, 3–6. The pressure and the stress from my previous matches were wearing me down and I felt myself dragging as I wiped the sweat from my eyes and prepared for the third set.

At 5–3, I had four chances for match point in the third, all opportunities on Steffi's own serve. But each chance, she turned me back. At the time, I didn't even realize I was playing for the match, so consumed was I with each point. All I knew was that I couldn't get control. With Steffi, there are few windows of opportunity and I wasted each one. Then, in the tenth game, Steffi broke my serve after I had made four unforced errors. Two hours plus into the match, Steffi and I were tied, 6 all.

The games continued to go back and forth until Steffi and I were tied, 8–8. I pulled ahead, 9–8. During the final game Steffi netted a forehand. I felt a rush of relief — point, game, set, match. Two hours and forty-three minutes after we'd begun, I'd won my third French Open.

"Good match," I said to Steffi as I shook her hand at the net.

I shook the umpire's hand, packed my tennis bag, and went to the press room for my interviews. "In a match like this when you are out there for so long and the last set is so close, in my opinion, both players deserve to win," I told the reporters. And I meant every word. Steffi had played a great match.

"What are your plans now?" one reporter asked.

"I've got some shopping to do," I said with a grin.

The following morning Mom and I went back to the Chanel boutique.

"Are you sure?" the saleswoman asked before she rang up the suit.

"I'm sure," I said to her. "Nobody is going to change my mind." In my life, people are always trying to influence me: what I say, what skirt I wear for tournaments, what brand of sneakers, soft drink, hair care products I like. This decision was all mine.

Whenever I open my closet and see the green Chanel suit hanging there, I'm reminded of my third French Open win. Since 1992 I've only worn that suit once, and then I felt it looked too grown up for me. It doesn't matter. One day that Chanel suit will be an antique. I'll wear it then.

There are some things a Chanel suit can't change. One of them was the press at 1992 Wimbledon.

After the French Open I packed my bags and headed for London. I was worried, but there was nothing I could do — I knew that the papers were going to get back at me for 1991. It didn't matter that I'd wanted to be there; that I'd been injured and couldn't have possibly played without hurting myself further. Skipping Wimbledon was an affront to the London press and, in their minds, to the English fans. Failing to explain my actions immediately had added insult to injury.

The London tabloids focused on the grunting. It was no longer just a strange quirk of my game, about which a few players had complained to the media; it had become an intentional act of distraction to break my opponent's concentration and irritate umpires. Nick Pitt wrote in the *Sunday Times*: "The images [Monica] conjures on court are certainly unattractive: a figure scuttling along the baseline like a crab; a face screwed up like a rodent's; a racket wielded like a hag with a frying pan; each blow . . . a grotesque double-handed mirror of the other punctuated by an exclamation from the torture chamber." Like the daughter of a cartoonist, I took Mr. Pitt's caricature of me in my stride. I understood the humor of his article — to me it was like a Benny Hill show.

I tried to ignore the tabloids and focus on the reason I was in London. Grand Slams are electric, bursting with barely managed egos, tempers, and desires. At Wimbledon in particular, tennis players get swept up in the hype and the prestige of the event. We always want to win, but we want to win Wimbledon more. Sometimes that obsession doesn't bring out the best in us. Unfortunately, some of my fellow players paid a little too much attention to the papers. Consciously or subconsciously, they used it against me during our matches.

Women's Rule 4.3.3. in the WTA Official Tour Book:

Hindrance Rule: Any unintentional delay of play, abuse of the 20-second rule or 90-second changeover shall subject a player to a warning on the first offense and a loss of point for all subsequent infractions thereafter. Any continual distraction of regular play, such as grunting, shall be dealt with as follows: the first offense will result in a let being called and the point being replayed; on the second offense, a let will be called, the point replayed and the player will be advised by the Chair Umpire that should there be a third or subsequent infraction, the infraction will result in a loss of point on each new occasion.

Nathalie Tauziat was the first to use the tabloids' obsession with my grunting against me. I'd played Nathalie in exhibitions and tournaments countless times. Not once had she complained about my grunting. We played against each other in the quarterfinals of Wimbledon. I took the first set easily, 6–1, and then we were tied, 3–3, in the second. In the middle of the match Nathalie walked over to the chair umpire and said something to him. What's going on? I wondered.

"Ms. Seles?" the umpire called. I walked over to his chair. "Ms. Tauziat is complaining about your noise." Hmmm, my noise. What was he talking about?

"Okay," I said and walked away. My noise? We started the next game, and I continued to play the way I always play. I didn't even think about my grunting. Halfway through the point Nathalie went back over to the umpire. I couldn't hear what she said, but I could tell that she was angry about something.

"Ms. Seles . . . ?"

"Yes, sir," I said as I walked back over to the umpire.

"If you don't tone it down, I will give you a warning," he said sternly.

"What are you talking about?" I asked. "You can't give me a warning for just playing my game. I'm not swearing, yelling, hitting my racket on the court."

"Ms. Seles, go back to playing or I'm going to give you a warning."

What Nathalie had done was unfair. She'd been given a window of opportunity by the tabloids to break my concentration during a match. She wanted to advance at Wimbledon and she didn't seem to care how she beat me. I'd been on my way to closing her out of the tournament, so she used her only weapon.

It was a frustrating feeling. I'd always grunted during matches. Always. All of a sudden I was getting warnings from the umpire; all of a sudden my opponent was complaining and disrupting my game. In the end, Nathalie's ploy worked against her. It made me mad and I just wanted to finish her off. I took control and quickly won the second set, 6–3. I shook Nathalie's hand after the match and said, "Good game."

I went to my post-match press conference. The first question was, what did I think about Ms. Tauziat's complaints? "It was surprising that someone I've played so many times picked this tournament to complain. I'm not certain it was coincidence that Nathalie was in trouble when she chose to complain about my grunting," I said.

The following morning assorted tabloid headlines read: "Seles Grunts and Players Can't Concentrate;" "Seles Almost Defaulted;" "Seles Fined for Grunting;" "We Won't Tolerate Grunts at Wimbledon." I tried not to care. It was the first time I had reached the semifinals at Wimbledon, and I was thrilled. I was scheduled to play Martina Navratilova. By then, Martina had won Wimbledon a record nine times in her career. Facing her on the grass would be a challenge. Not only was she favored, but the crowd was strongly behind their champion.

I took the first set, 6–2. The games were closer and tougher than the score reflected. The second set was even more of a battle. We finally reached 6–6, which meant a tie-breaker against an equal player. Focus, Monica, I told myself as Martina's left-handed serve whizzed across the net. But moments later, not even I could keep my mind on the game. Martina left the baseline and went over to the umpire. I couldn't hear what she said, because the umpire covered his microphone. I was called over to the chair.

"Ms. Seles, Ms. Navratilova has complained about your noise. Please tone it down," the umpire said.

"Fine," I replied. "Just fine."

I walked back to the baseline. This is never going to end now, I thought with frustration. Martina won the tie-breaker, 7–3. We started the third set, and I felt my game slide back into place. That's when Martina went back over to the umpire. This time the microphone wasn't completely covered. I heard the words "grunting," and "pig." Once again, I was called over and told to be quieter. I returned to the court and took the third set, 6–4, to win the match. I was going to play my first finals match at Wimbledon against Steffi Graf. Complaints or not, I was ecstatic.

Martina had lost, so she went to the press conference first. I went to the locker room and changed into a dry shirt so that I wouldn't get chilled. Then I walked up the steps to the conference. Martina was on her way down.

"Monica, can I talk to you for a minute?" she asked.

"Sure," I replied.

"I just want to apologize for what I said on the court. I was caught up in the heat of the moment. I know I can't take it back, but I'm sorry," Martina said quietly.

At that point I wasn't even certain what Martina had said to the umpire, because I couldn't hear her complaint clearly. In a few minutes the press would tell me that she'd compared my grunting to a pig being cut in a butcher shop. Still, I wasn't upset with her. Martina didn't complain because she wanted to win by breaking my concentration. She was too good a player for that. I don't know for certain, but I believe that, as she felt the game slipping, she began to focus on my grunting. Like a dripping faucet, it got to her. I appreciated her apology: she'd come to say sorry to me personally instead of sending a note through her agent.

The next morning the papers zeroed in on my grunting with this quote from Martina: "It just gets louder and louder. You cannot hear the ball being hit . . . I am not saying I lost because of her grunting. I would have said this if I won . . . I know she is not doing it on purpose, but she can stop it on purpose."

No one backed me up — not the other players, the press, or an official from the WTA. I was the number one player in the world, about to play in the finals at Wimbledon, and I was being attacked from all quarters. Commentators on television were discussing whether or not I should be fined or banned from tennis for my grunting. Tabloids were printing untrue stories. The upmarket newspapers were writing cruel articles and I knew I couldn't take much more, so I decided to change: I would hold my breath in after I hit the ball instead of exhaling with the force.

When I stepped onto center court to play Steffi Graf in the Wimbledon finals, I only thought about one thing: Don't grunt. It was one of the biggest mistakes I've ever made. Concentrating on something as stupid as grunting during a Grand Slam final — what was I thinking? The truth is that I wasn't. I was just reacting.

Steffi and I played in the rain, which forced three delays and prolonged the finals match to five and a half hours. The actual playing time only lasted fifty-eight minutes. I never got into the match, never had the chance to win. I lost the first set, 6–2; the second, 6–1. More than anything, I was disappointed in myself. No one had made me stop grunting for the finals: I'd made that decision; I'd been the one to fold under the pressure.

My father had tried to warn me. "Monica, you've got to go with your game style," he said. "You can't listen to everybody. You cannot satisfy them all. They've either got to accept you the way you are, or not." He was right. But I was eighteen years old, and I wanted people to like me. For the past month I'd been kicked and criticized to the point of breaking. Even after I stopped reading the articles, the headlines flashed at me from every grocery store, every shop counter. I wasn't the only target of the tabloids: Steffi received her fair share. But those articles focused on her father's problems, not on her as an individual.

"Why couldn't they just let me enjoy getting to my first Wimbledon finals?" I asked my dad after the match. He didn't have an answer.

The first time—hitting in 1978, aged only five, with my brother Zoltan

A portrait of me on the courts by my father, a professional cartoonist who drew me pictures to make tennis lessons fun

Posing in front of the apartment wall where I learned to hit

First day at school

Above right:
Almost ready
to play

Is this racket big enough?

Going after the ball in 1981

Dad gives me some pointers as we watch Zoltan play a match

Indoor practice

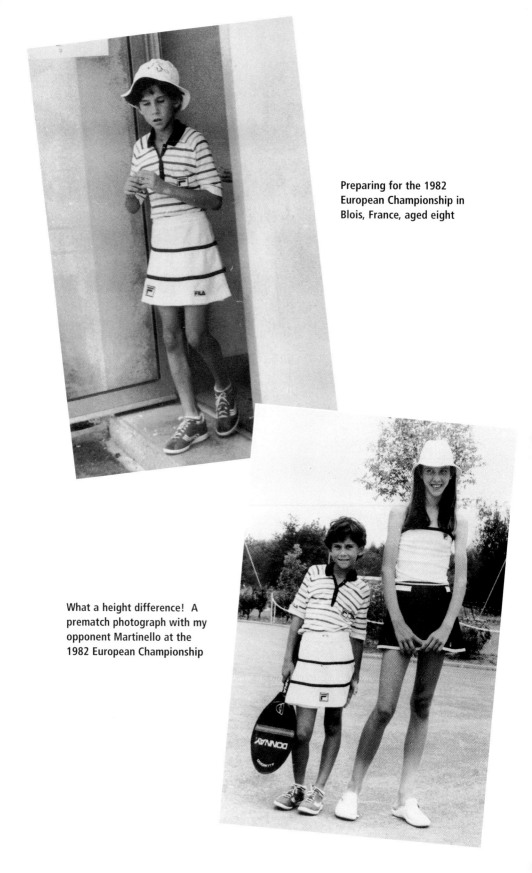

Preparing for the 1982
European Championship in
Blois, France, aged eight

What a height difference! A
prematch photograph with my
opponent Martinello at the
1982 European Championship

Warming up with Zoltan

My first win at the 1982
European Nationals

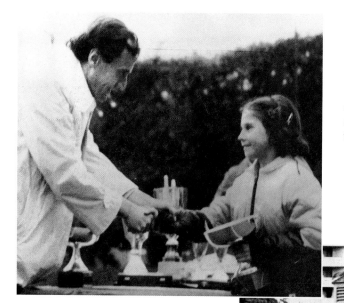

A handshake and a trophy at an International Italian tournament in 1983

The coach and his student—with my father in 1984 at the Disney Sport Goofy tournament

My first big tournament check

1989—my first time on grass

With good friend Betsy Nagelsen
at the McCormack's home in 1990

Practice on the public courts in 1990. Despite being a top professional player, I had nowhere else to go when I was told I could no longer train at the Bollettieri Academy

The 1989 French Open—the stadium of my dreams

Shaking hands with Steffi Graf having beaten her in the 1990 French Open to take my first Grand Slam title

A moment of glory: beating Martina Navratilova to take the US Open in September 1991

Center of attention:
(Above) proudly
displaying to the
Press the US Open
Trophy, which I won
for the second time
in September 1992

And, *(left)* in January
1993, the Australian
Open trophy I had
won for the third
consecutive year

Giving a tennis lesson
at the Special Olympics
in 1995

With Astro in Vail in
1993 during my recovery
from the attack

With my agent Mark McCormack and my mother on the way to the 1995 Atlantic City Exhibition, my first public game since the attack

A warm gesture of support from Martina Navratilova after the Atlantic City Exhibition

Sharing the happiness at my
return to tennis: *(right)* reaching
around a police guard to shake
hands with a supporter at
Atlantic City and *(below)* signing
autographs for tennis enthusiasts
at the US Open, September 1995

At the 1996 Special Olympics with Sonya Bell, the thirteen-year-old blind gymnast whose determination and fortitude inspired me

Enjoying myself at a nightclub with Anke Huber and Mary Joe Fernandez after the 1996 Australian Open

$$\left(35\right)$$

By the time the 1992 US Open came around, I was a little down. The day before my first round I sat in the stands at Flushing Meadows and watched some of the other players practice. At some point, as I've mentioned, Arthur Ashe sat down beside me and we began to talk. There had always been something about Arthur that made me feel comfortable. I'd never been afraid to tell him how I was doing, because he wouldn't use my vulnerability against me. It just wasn't his nature. That afternoon I told him how the press had been ripping me apart for my grunting — how it was hurting my game and my feelings.

"Monica, you have to believe in yourself and your own strength," he said softly. "Don't think about Wimbledon, or why the tabloids have been writing negative stories about you. Just focus on your game and go with the flow."

I stared into Arthur's soft brown eyes. Here was a man who had been knocked down countless times. Born in Virginia in 1943, when racial segregation was the law, he had loved tennis, but couldn't play in any of the junior tournaments because he was black. It took lobbying for him even to be admitted into the previously segregated US Interscholastic tournament in 1961, which he won. He went on to attend the University of California at Los Angeles, and to lead their varsity team to the US Intercollegiate singles title.

Segregation was eventually outlawed, and Arthur became a professional tennis player. Even then, he came up against a lot of people who didn't think he belonged in the sport. He never gave up, though, and in 1975 he won Wimbledon and became the US number one and the world number four player. A major heart attack forced him to retire from the sport he loved in 1979. But, even after the media found out he had AIDS and told the world, his spirit remained gentle and true. "Just believe in yourself," Arthur said that day in the stands.

Arthur Ashe will never know how much his words meant to me. I repeated them in my head throughout the Open, and they helped at a time when I needed to know that someone believed in me. By the time I reached the semifinals, I hadn't dropped a set. I played Mary Joe Fernandez in the semis and beat her, 6–3, 6–2. In the finals I faced Arantxa Sanchez Vicario, who'd beaten Steffi Graf in straight sets the previous round. I took the finals easily, 6–3, 6–3, to win my second US Open Grand Slam.

I left that tournament pleased with my game, and my mindset. Arthur had been right. Nothing mattered but what *I* thought. The papers would no doubt upset me again in the future, but I knew that what mattered was what I believed in. I had to let go of everything else. That takes a lot of strength.

36

Strength. It surged through me in the end of 1992, and carried me into January of 1993. But no matter how strong I felt, I still couldn't move my neck after more than twenty hours on a plane to the Australian Open. The tournament director suggested I see a chiropractor in Melbourne. I had to do something, so I agreed.

I had never been to a chiropractor before. I lay on the examining table and looked over at my mother. When the chiropractor slowly turned my head and then whipped it back in the opposite direction, I don't know which of us was more frightened. My neck popped and cracked loudly. "One more time," the man said. He turned my head at an angle, and then snapped it back again. *Crack.* It took three more days before it felt better, and it would probably have been better by then anyway. Next time, I'll wait.

Australia might have started off with a little discomfort, but it ended up being the most enjoyable Grand Slam I'd ever had. My entire family came with me — even my brother, who hadn't traveled with me for some time. We decided to stay in our own apartment in the town of Melbourne, instead of in the large center near the stadium. It was the difference between staying at the Plaza hotel in New York and a little place in Greenwich Village. I loved it!

A childhood friend was living in Melbourne, and she took me all over town before the tournament began. We spent a lot of time window shopping in fun stores, hitting the popular restaurants, even visiting dance halls. We also spent time in the parks, just sitting in the sunshine and talking. It felt more like a vacation than the lead-up to a Grand Slam.

I moved through my early rounds easily. In the quarterfinals I had to play against Julie Halard from France. She's a good player, and my nerves buzzed a bit as I stepped onto the court. I took the first set, 6–2, but she fought for the second and won, 6–7. Take control, Monica, I said to myself at the start of the third set. I won the set, 6–0, and moved to the semifinals.

The semifinal of the Australian Open was one of the easiest matches I've ever played against Gabriela Sabatini. I took the first set, 6–1, and the second, 6–2. I played some great tennis, and began to feel a sense of balance I hadn't regained since becoming the world number one.

As much as I hate to admit it, reaching the top changed more than my ranking on a piece of paper and the attitude of the media. It's hard to be in a position where you feel that you're constantly defending yourself. Climbing up the ladder is easier than sitting at the top waiting for someone to push you off. Being number one was never my goal, but once I was there I wasn't eager to have it taken away. At first, I was playing defensively in order to preserve my position. But at the 1993 Australian Open I was once again just playing my game.

I faced Steffi Graf in the finals. She took the first set, 4–6, but I still felt my momentum building. I took the second set, 6–3, and the third, 6–2. I was excited to have won my third Australian Open. But I remember that I was more excited by how I'd won it: I'd spent a week enjoying Melbourne before the tournament, sightseeing and relaxing with friends and family; I'd moved through my early rounds with confidence and determination; and, most importantly, I'd finally been able to change my mindset — to forget about rank and reputation and just play for sheer enjoyment.

After the Australian I returned to the US and played a Virginia Slims tournament in Chicago. In the spring of '91 I'd lost in the first round of the same tournament. At the time, I thought my game was going downhill, but I had come back that year to win the Australian, French, and US Open. This time, I won the Chicago tournament.

"Thank you for letting me make up for the last time I played in

Chicago," I said at the awards ceremony. "I'm hoping this is a positive sign that the rest of 1993 will be a great year for me." I couldn't have been more wrong. After losing in 1991, I climbed up from the bottom of the barrel. In 1993 I was on top . . . I should have seen that the only way to go was down.

I flew to a tournament in Paris straight from Chicago. I was already beginning to feel run down because of the temperature difference between Australia and freezing Chicago. In Paris it was cold and rainy. I began to get sick, but I still wanted to play doubles with Betsy Nagelsen. Our first round was the night before my quarterfinals singles match.

We didn't start until 11:00 pm. We took the first set, 6–4, and lost the second, 4–6. By then, it was already 1:00 am. Betsy and I really wanted to win, regardless of the time. We're both very competitive players, and neither of us will let a match go until the handshake at the net. The third set went back and forth, and in the end we lost. It was 2:00 am. I wouldn't get into my hotel bed until three in the morning. I had a quarterfinals match at 11:00 am that same day.

The match wasn't memorable. I played Mary Pierce and won, 6–2, 6–2. Adrenalin helped me to stay focused during play, but when it was over I felt exhaustion beginning to creep into my bones. There wasn't time to rest. I played Conchita Martinez in the semifinals and won, 6–1, 6–1.

Unfortunately, the finals weren't as easy to dominate. I faced Martina Navratilova. I took the first set, 6–3, and she won the second, 4–6. I felt sick as we began the third. To this day, I'm not sure how I won it. All I remember about the match is that my head felt light and my lungs hurt when I ran. I left Paris the next morning.

Immediately after my return to Florida I went to see a doctor. He told me I had a nasty viral infection and prescribed total relaxation. I pulled out of my next few tournaments and took a flight to Jamaica with Zoltan. I lay on the warm sands and let the sun and heat radiate through my body. I hadn't known how exhausted I was from travel and tournaments until I let myself sleep hour after hour on the beach. After a week we flew home and I continued to recuperate through March and early April.

The French Open was only a month away by the time I was well enough to play tennis again. I had the chance to win my fourth consecutive French Open — something that had never been done before — I knew that I needed to enter at least one tournament before the Grand Slam began. Originally I chose a tournament in Barcelona; however, I had to pull out because I still wasn't strong enough to play. That left the Citizen Cup in Hamburg. My only reservation was that I'd had problems there in 1991.

The last time I went to Germany for a tournament I was served court papers as I tried to get out of my car at the hotel. The man with the papers spoke no English, and I didn't speak German. He came toward me very quickly, and I got scared and jumped back inside the car. As the man leapt forward to reach me, he struck the car and almost caught my arm in the swinging door. At that point I had no security, so the German driver interceded and finally took the papers from the man. They were from a German firm which had represented me as a child player in Yugoslavia. The agency had decided to sue me because I had chosen different representation when I moved to the United States.

I tried to remind myself that the incident had nothing to do with tennis, and that the Citizen Cup would be a good tournament to play before the French Open. Put things in perspective, Monica, I reminded myself.

I requested a wild card four days before the start of the Hamburg tournament. A wild card is an admission into a tournament for a player who hadn't originally planned to play that tournament. There are a predetermined number of slots reserved for wild cards. They usually go either to well-known players whose rankings are not high enough to gain admission to the tournament but who are still attractions, or to top players who decide to enter at the last minute. Since I'd pulled out of Barcelona so late, I hadn't been entered for the Citizen Cup and therefore needed a wild card to play, which was granted by the tournament director. Ironically, had I not been too sick to play in Barcelona, I never would have played in Hamburg.

But I didn't know back then what I know now. In April of 1993 I believed that things were looking up. I was healthy, strong, and ready to play.

$$\left(\!\!\!\!\begin{array}{c} 37 \end{array}\!\!\!\!\right)$$

If there's one thing I learned in April 1993, it's that no one is invincible. When I look back now to the week of the Citizen Cup in Hamburg, I think how naive I was: how foolish to think that nothing could stop me from continuing to play my game and win tournaments. Now I know better. And I understand that it was only after accepting help from professionals, family and friends that I was able to rebuild my life.

I spent the anniversary of the Hamburg stabbing with Betsy Nagelsen and her brother, Jimmy. On April 30, 1994, I drove down to Orlando to watch the NBA playoffs. We had tickets to see the game live, but I didn't want to appear in public that day. Betsy and Jimmy understood. Instead, we went into the library at Betsy's house, closed all the blinds, and made three beds out of couches. Then we brought in plates of junk food and pigged out while we watched the game. It wasn't the healthiest thing to do, but I felt safe, comfortable, and happy to be in the company of friends. Every once in a while, I'd think: It's been a year since Hamburg. Then I'd focus on the game, and the love and laughter in that room.

I stayed the night at Betsy's, and the next morning she and Jimmy got me up early and took me for a run. "Boot camp today to make up for yesterday's eating," Betsy laughed as she pulled me out of bed. I didn't stop running and biking until late that afternoon, when I sat by the pool while Betsy swam laps. I was just enjoying the sunshine, my mind no longer dwelling on the attack.

"Monica," Jimmy said as he walked over, "I have some sad news."

"Oh boy," I said under my breath. "What now?"

"Ayrton Senna just died in a racing accident," Jimmy said in a broken voice.

Ayrton had been my favorite Formula One driver. I'd spent an afternoon talking to him in his trailer when I visited him in Italy in 1993. He'd been so understanding and kind. Ayrton had a way of looking on the positive side, and believed in living every second of every day. "You're so lucky," I said to him. "You're doing something you love, and you never have to be scared like I am now."

"Well, Monica," he had replied, "I've never been stabbed or hurt in my sport, so I can't imagine how that feels. Still, when I drive my car through a turn, I've known fear, but I know that it's something I have to go through because afterward I'll feel great." I am going to die sooner than he is, I had thought when I left the trailer.

It had been a year since my attack, and I still wasn't living a full life. And now Ayrton, who'd lived each minute like it was his last, was gone. I'd been given the gift of time, and as I sat by Betsy's pool I promised myself that I would use that gift; that by next year I would be living a full life.

"I can't believe how much better I feel when I practice," I told Dr. May when I returned to Tahoe in June for more therapy.

"You get your joy from tennis," he said. "Whether or not you play competitively again, you love the game and you have to play for yourself. Now, how are you doing?"

"I'm still seeing his face," I confided. "Parche is like a dark force in my life. He's overpowering . . . and the knife, I see the knife every night, and I smell the bloody shirt . . ."

Dr. May listened quietly as I let my emotions spill out. "You can't control what happened in Hamburg," he said finally. "You can use the techniques we've worked on to give you a realistic sense of control, but that doesn't change what's happened in the past. You've got to accept that in order to move on. You've committed to therapy, that's the first step. Now you need to understand your emotional reactions to the attack, Parche, your life. That's going to reduce your depression, and help you to find the joy in life again."

I saw Dr. May for long periods during the summer. When I was home, I tried to work on my goals, use the techniques I'd learned, play tennis, and curb my eating. Some days were good, some bad. But I was making progress.

In November Stephanie Tolleson called. "Monica, I normally wouldn't bother you with this kind of stuff," she said, "but I thought you might be interested to know that you've been invited to present at the Arete Awards for the most courageous young athlete of the year. The award is going to Sonya Bell; she's a thirteen-year-old blind gymnast. You're her hero."

"Let me think about it, Stephanie," I said.

The idea that I was someone's hero — especially a girl who was only seven years younger than me — was strange. I wanted to meet her, and to do something for an athlete who was so brave: this girl did somersaults on the balance beam, technical floor routines, swung from the uneven bars!

"I'll do it," I told Stephanie two hours later. "But I don't want anyone to know I've accepted until the day of the awards, and security has to be really tight." It would be my first public appearance in over a year. I was very nervous, but I was going anyway.

My mother flew with me to the award ceremony in Chicago. I walked into the banquet hall for the rehearsal at 2:00 in the afternoon. There were a few people on stage going through their presentations, and several more sitting in the audience listening. I knew people were shocked to see me walk onto the stage to run through my speech. Not even the guest of honor, Sonya, knew that I'd agreed to come and present her award. When I had finished, I walked past a table where a young girl and her parents were sitting. I didn't know she was Sonya until her parents called me to their table and introduced us.

"Hi, are you Monica?" the gymnast asked shyly.

"Hello, Sonya," I said. "I'm Monica Seles . . ."

Sonya leapt to her feet and hugged me. "I watch you all the time," she said breathlessly. "I know it's you because I can hear you grunting." (Finally, someone appreciated my grunts!) "I'm so happy you came — I can't believe you're here — it means everything to me!" I stayed for the next hour and talked with Sonya about school, friends, life. I told her that her determination and bravery were an inspiration to me. I don't know if she believed me, but I meant every word.

The Arete Awards were held that night. The whole evening was very special. I presented Sonya's award, and heard many other athletes talking about overcoming adversity. Baseball player Hank Aaron, who was at the awards, came over to talk to me and give me some words of encouragement. He even mentioned me in his presentation, which meant so much to me. At the end of the evening, for the first time in almost a year, I spoke briefly to the press. I kept my comments short and vague, for I still didn't have any answers.

38

He sat on the sidewalk beneath the blue cloth awning of a large department store. He wore green fatigues, dark with dirt and the rain that had been falling for days. A large white plastic bag was wrapped around his torso — a makeshift raincoat. Beside him sat a medium-sized dog — no particular breed, just a brown mutt, cute because of his unlikely mix. In the dog's mouth was a cup. I wanted to put money in it, but I was afraid because I didn't know the dog. I watched a lady drop a few coins into the container, so I walked over and reached into my pocket. The man didn't look up as the coins clinked into the cup, but the dog did, and his eyes were large, sad, and without hope.

My mother and I went into the store in Seattle. We'd come to the city in late November of '94 to visit a friend of mine — part of my attempt to begin living again. Neither of us had expected to be sitting on a bench in the store thinking about a man and his dog.

"Did you see their faces?" I asked my mom. "They looked broken . . . The dog's eyes were so sad . . . maybe I can take him home with me."

"You can't do that, Monica. That dog is probably the only thing the man has in his life to love," she said.

I spent that night thinking about the man and his dog and trying to come up with a solution for them. I thought how hard it must be to be a homeless person: how could he get a job, if he had no address to put down on an application, no telephone number where he could be contacted?

The next morning I went back to the store in search of the pair.

"How are you, sir?" I asked tentatively as I stood before the man beneath the blue cloth awning. "Are you cold?"

"Yeah," he replied. "We've been out here a long time."

I bought two coffees and returned to sit down beside him. We started to talk. The guy had no idea who I was, but I told him that I understood what it was like to be depressed. "I was a tennis player," I said, "but then I got stabbed during a match." I don't know why I told him that; I'm not usually so open. It just felt appropriate.

"You don't look like someone who would get stabbed," the man said in surprise. "But at least you came through it and went on with your life. I'm a Vietnam vet, and I can't seem to let go of the war . . ."

"Well, I haven't let go of the stabbing," I confided. "Every day I fight to get past it, but I haven't yet."

We talked for almost an hour. When it was time to leave, I wasn't sure how to go. It broke my heart to leave the man and his dog out there in the rain and cold. In the end I handed him some cash.

"I can't accept this," the man said, in shock. "There's too much here!"

"Sir, I am leaving Seattle tomorrow and I will probably never see you again. Please take the money; I want you to have it. All I ask is that you promise me you won't buy alcohol or cigarettes, and that you'll buy your dog some good food. He's so sweet. I'd take him back with me in a second."

"I promise," the man said. "And I'd give you my dog if I could, but he's my lifeline. He is the only one I can talk to, the only one I can hug."

It was so hard to walk away from them. I don't want to be like that, I thought. I've got to start focusing on the present, otherwise I'll be stuck in the past, too. No more "tomorrow I'll get on the court — tomorrow I'll start exercising — tomorrow I'll stop letting Parche's actions control me." There was only *now*. I was weeks away from my twenty-first birthday. It was time to live again.

39

It was a day I'd looked forward to since I was sixteen. Twenty-one was the age of freedom. I'd be able to go anywhere I wanted — to pubs and nightclubs, but it wasn't just the idea of being able to drink legally; it was more that age would no longer be an issue.

Unfortunately, life doesn't always turn out as you think it will. That goes for birthdays, too. When I returned from Seattle I began to go through the motions of training and practicing, but even though I'd set my mind to living in the present, the past kept interfering. Dr. May had told me that I'd have good times and bad times, but I was ready for more good than bad. I was ready for the nightmare to end. Frustration overwhelmed me, and my mood began to plunge.

"Monica, do you think you should maybe go for a little run?" my father asked when he saw I wasn't exercising much. "And then we could hit for a little while . . ."

"I can't do this!" I cried and stormed out of the room. I began to think in terms of "tomorrow" again. "Tomorrow, I'll run four miles. Tomorrow I'll stop eating 5,000 calories a day. Tomorrow, tomorrow, tomorrow."

"Monica, what do you want to do for your birthday?" my mother asked on November 30, two days beforehand.

"Nothing," I replied. "I don't want to celebrate it this year. There is nothing to celebrate. And I don't want any presents — I don't want anything from anyone."

"Please let us do something little," Mom said. "Just let us buy you a gift and have a little party."

"No."

On December 2, 1994, I turned twenty-one years old. When I woke up, I knew it would be a bad day. "Everything is rotten," I grumbled as I got out of bed.

My parents and Zoltan couldn't bear not to celebrate my birthday. They got me a cake with candles. "Make a wish," my mother said as I stared down at the burning candles. When I was a kid, I was very superstitious: I wouldn't step on a crack, hurt insects or refuse wishes. But on my twenty-first birthday I wanted to scream that I no longer believed in wishes — that wishing for anything made no sense. Instead, I closed my eyes and blew out the candles. My father handed me a gift from our family. I opened the small box and took out a simple gold bracelet.

"Your life has been so complicated that we thought we'd buy you a simple gift," he explained as he fastened the single band around my wrist. "We hope that in this next year there will be no more complications."

I hadn't wanted a gift, but the sentiment was so pure and loving that I couldn't be angry. A few days later my mood began to lighten again, and I went to see Dr. May with hopes that things might get better. And they did.

By Christmas time, I had begun to train in earnest. Once again my father and I played every day, and as my therapy progressed, my eating habits were slowly changing and I was starting to lose weight. In addition, I felt like celebrating the holidays.

My parents decided they wanted to buy me another bracelet for Christmas. This time, they picked out two different ones, and then asked which I'd prefer. One gold bracelet had turtles connecting each band. The other had ladybugs.

"Turtles are a symbol of long life," my mother explained.

"And ladybugs are good luck," Dad added. "Which do you want, Monica?"

I chose the turtle. I didn't believe in luck anymore, but I believed that if you lived long enough, you could get through just about anything.

*   *   *

In January of '95 I returned to see Dr. May. We talked about the scream I kept hearing in my head.

"Maybe you should watch the tape of the attack," he suggested. "That way you'll be able to put the scream in its place — move on to the next level."

I agreed. When I returned to Sarasota my parents and I played the tape of my match in Hamburg.

I'm not sorry I watched it — only that I watched it at night, which gave it an eerie, dream-like quality. There I was playing Maleeva, fighting to stay in the match. Then it was time for the changeover. The camera-man moved from the players to the stands. There was a scream — it sounded like a wounded animal. The camera swung up to the Citizen Cup sign. When it swung back, I was walking forward toward the net, holding my back. Parche was being restrained by several men. His face was contorted and red, his arm twisted behind his back at a severe angle. I stumbled forward and a man appeared behind me. He put his hands on my shoulders, and I fell back into his arms. The look on my face never changed. It was a look of utter shock and betrayal.

I leapt up from the couch and left the den. I couldn't watch anymore. I couldn't control the irrational thoughts that were speeding through my mind. Positive thoughts, Monica, I thought as my hysteria grew. Positive thoughts. It was a tough night, but Dr. May had been right. Watching the attack and hearing the scream that had echoed through my head so many nights eventually helped me to move on.

A few weeks later I turned on ESPN and watched some tennis matches. I listened to the spectators cheering the players, and I thought about my practices in the backyard with my dad. There was no excitement: when I hit a winner, there was no reaction. I missed that.

"Dad, I want to play on the tennis courts at the clubhouse in our development," I said one morning. "Let's get a few guys for me to play that I'm comfortable with and have known for a while." My dad was speechless. "I'm ready to make this step," I said with a nervous smile.

That evening I went out and hit on the club courts. There were several people playing tennis, and after I finished practicing they came up and said, "It's great to see you, Monica. We hope you'll beat this thing and come back."

For the first time, I didn't cry.

40

In late February 1995 Martina Navratilova called me. She was coming down to Fort Myers, Florida, to play in the Federation Cup. "Monica, I haven't practiced for a long time, would you mind if I came over to visit you and maybe we could hit for a while?"

"Okay, sure," I said in surprise.

Martina arrived at my home with her Fox Terrier, KD. KD stands for Killer Dog, which is a funny name for such a tiny animal but very appropriate. I remember one US Open when my locker was right below Martina's. She'd left KD in the locker room while she played, and when I went in to get my things the dog wouldn't let me near my locker. I had to get ready for a match, but I couldn't because KD would have bitten me if I'd tried to open my locker. Finally I called an attendant to move the dog so that I could change.

Martina and I had a great time. We hit a bit on my court in the morning, and she even gave me some tips on volleys. After practice we bounced on my trampoline. It was amazing to see Martina, who I knew first as an idol, playing like a little kid. When we took a break to get some lunch, Martina said, "You know, Monica, we'd all love to have you back on the tour. It has to be your decision, but I just want you to know that everyone would welcome you with open arms."

I really appreciated Martina's words, and her sincerity. When it was time for her to leave, she unclasped a beautiful gold bracelet from her wrist and handed it to me. "Monica, I want you to have this. It has brought me a lot of luck." She hooked the bracelet around my wrist.

"Martina, I can't accept this," I said in wonder.

"When you come back, you can return it to me," she said with a smile.

"What if I never come back?" I asked.

"Then you'll never return it. But it will still bring you luck."

Martina is an incredibly generous person. On the court she's tough, but in real life she has a huge heart. What if I could never return her bracelet? I thought after she'd left. Or worse, what if I lost it?

I only wore that bracelet once over the next few months. But I'd look at it often, especially when the nightmares made sleep impossible and left me feeling hopeless. Slowly, I began to think about my comeback. Maybe it was the bracelet, or maybe it was just time to move on. I like to think it was a little bit of both.

41

I began hinting about a comeback to my friend, Betsy, in mid-March. But I was afraid to say the words, "I want to play professional tennis again." How would I return to the game? There were so many issues, concerns, involved parties, decisions. I couldn't figure them out alone. Although my parents supported my decision, they couldn't help me to decide the best way to play professional tennis again. Betsy could see what I wanted, so she suggested I talk to her husband. Mark McCormack is really good at rolling up his sleeves and figuring out situations. Luckily, he wanted to help me.

I drove down to Orlando with my father to meet with Mark. My dad brought a letter he'd written, which began:

> I think we have to put the attack behind us and move on, and I would like to ask you, as the head of IMG, to help me do that with my daughter. We really would like it if you can help us sort through several issues, including the sponsor lawsuit and Monica's potential suit against the German Tennis Federation for inadequate security. In addition, we would like to reimburse IMG for every-thing that they have done for Monica in the past two years, during which time IMG hasn't been paid because they have received no commissions . . .

I met with Mark alone. "The most important thing is that you do what makes you happy," Mark said after we'd talked at length. "Financi-ally, you don't ever need to pick up a racket again. You have the freedom to do whatever you want with your life. Do you really want to return to professional tennis?"

"Yes," I replied. And as I said the word, I knew I really meant it. "But how?"

"Monica, I'd love to accept the challenge of sorting out your problems and getting you back into the game," Mark said with a smile. He told me he'd go to Italy to meet with the head of one of my sponsors to try to resolve our differences. He would also visit the German Tennis Federation. As far as reimbursing IMG, he said he'd get back to us with a number.

"If this is what you want to do," Mark said, "then I think it's really important to develop a step-by-step plan for your comeback. First, you need to start practicing hard, because from what I understand you've been playing sporadically. Second, because you haven't played a professional match in two years, I think it's important that you start with an exhibition match. In an exhibition, we can control the environment — pick the stadium, and the size of the crowd, maintain security. You also won't have to worry about losing points or rank."

"I agree one hundred percent," I found myself saying.

"Okay, then let's tentatively plan for a comeback around Wimbledon time — July of 1995," Mark said. "Let's leave this meeting with both of us thinking that you're going to walk out on a tennis court in four months."

That night Betsy, Mark, my father and I had dinner together. We talked about the comeback; at one point we touched on security measures. My father made the comment, "It's like Monica is sitting in a chair with two buttons. Push one button and she earns a million dollars. Push the other and she dies." The reality of the situation hit me like a truck, and I excused myself and went to the bathroom. I felt the tears coming, and there was nothing I could do to stop them. *Is this the right decision?* I wondered. *Is tennis worth risking my life for?*

I've never played tennis for the money, and it didn't influence my decision now. So why was I going to return? I asked myself. In the end my decision had nothing to do with Parche. I wasn't returning to tennis to show him that he hadn't won; nor was I trying to prove that he no longer scared me, because he still did. I simply had an overwhelming desire to play professional tennis again — to face some of the greatest players in the world and battle it out on center court. I splashed cold water on my face and returned to the dinner table. It was time to live again.

When I left Orlando and returned home, I began to practice every day, training and working on my diet. By the end of March my game was in good shape, and I felt stronger than I'd felt in years. I was getting ready to step back onto a professional tennis court and into my life. And Günther Parche was getting ready for his second trial. I was certain that the German people would still be outraged by his actions and refuse to allow him to go unpunished.

But the atmosphere had changed in Germany by the time Parche was charged a second time. My feeling was that some of the German papers had made a 180-degree switch and, instead of criticizing the first verdict and supporting the second trial, they began to attack me. I was a big tennis star prosecuting a poor, misguided "lamb" who hadn't really meant to hurt anyone. The shift made me uneasy, but I still assumed that my lawyers would make sure Parche was found guilty.

A week before the second trial in April 1995 my lawyer called. "Monica, I think it's important for you to come to Germany to testify against Parche," he said. "The judge needs to understand the emotional damage that Parche inflicted."

It wasn't enough that Parche had stabbed me on a tennis court before 10,000 spectators. It wasn't enough that he'd admitted his guilt. Now I had to go to Germany and share the intimate details of my recovery. Worse, the way in which the German court was designed meant that I would have to sit at the prosecutor's table with my back to Parche while I testified. I just couldn't do it.

"I'll ask Dr. May to go to Germany for the trial and testify on my behalf about my emotional suffering," I told my lawyer. He wasn't happy with the decision, but it was the best I could do.

Dr. May agreed to go to Germany. During the trial he testified about my state of mind: "She is fearful, cries and feels very nervous. She is not sleeping well and has nightmares. She's frightened that Mr. Parche could attack her again." He called after his testimony to say I'd made the right decision. Sitting with my back to Parche while I relived the attack would have been too much to ask of me at that point.

Meanwhile, I focused on my comeback. I flew to William and Mary College at the beginning of April for the dedication of a tennis center named for Mark McCormack and Betsy. It was a great trip, and I even practiced on the new center's courts. When my mother and I left for the airport to return home, we were both feeling happy and confident. I rang Stephanie Tolleson from the airport.

"Stephanie, it's Monica," I said lightly. "Anything going on?"

"I have some bad news, Monica," Stephanie said. "Parche is free again."

On April 3, 1995, Parche's suspended sentence and two-year probation from the first trial was upheld. The appellate judge stated that a harsher sentence wasn't justified because of Parche's full confession. "Our law does not function on the principle 'an eye for an eye,'" she stated. Despite a court-appointed psychiatrist's testimony that Parche was "a perverse, scurrilous loner . . ." he was free.

I hung up the phone and fell into my mother's arms. I couldn't stop crying. Stephanie had said that my German lawyer Dr. Danelzik was going to file a last appeal and attempt to try Parche again, but I couldn't think about that. I couldn't think about anything but my own fear. "Let's get out of here," I said to my mom. We left the airport and hopped into a cab. I told the cabby to drive anywhere.

"Are you all right?" the man asked as he pulled away from the curb.

"Just drive," I said softly. I don't know where we went, only that we were in that cab for hours. Monica, you are obviously not going to get justice, I told myself when the shock had worn off. So you have two choices — return to tennis or go and do something else. Whatever you do, you have to let this go and move on.

My mom and I got a hotel room, and flew back to Sarasota the following day.

I called Mark McCormack a few weeks later. "Who do you have in mind for me to play at the exhibition?" I asked. If he was surprised to hear from me, he didn't say.

"How about Martina?" he asked.

"Sure. That would be great," I replied.

$$\left(42\right)$$

"I think you should go to the French Open in June. It's a great opportunity to meet with the WTA and several other groups who will be involved in your return to professional tennis," Mark McCormack suggested.

"That's a good idea," I agreed.

"Monica, I know that you were involved with the Special Olympics before the attack," he went on. "Do you want to continue your relationship with them?"

"Definitely, I want to continue that," I said.

"Well, the World Games are scheduled for the first week in July. It's the biggest sporting event on the planet in '95," Mark explained. "I'll make the arrangements."

I practiced until a week before the French Open. Before I flew to Paris I went down to Miami to try out several new Yonex rackets. Throughout my ordeal Yonex as a company was incredibly supportive and, as people, extremely considerate. After the practice with Yonex, I headed to the airport with my manager, Tony Godsick (who works with Stephanie) and my mother. While I was checking in, I felt a soft tap on my shoulder.

We hadn't told anyone that I'd be at the French Open. I was going for business and, since I wasn't playing in the Grand Slam, I didn't really want anyone to know I was in Paris. It wouldn't be fair to the other players to take attention away from their games. When I turned round and saw Chris Evert, my heart sank. She was a television commentator now, and my trip to Paris during the French Open would provide an interesting topic of conversation during the matches. Chris was surprised to see me, but she didn't ask why I was going to Paris.

Everything went well when we arrived in France. We got our luggage and headed to the hotel. No one recognized me, and there were no journalists around. Around noon my mother and I decided to take a walk and, as we stepped out of the hotel, two photographers ran forward. They'd been waiting for me — somehow they'd learned that I was in Paris. Great, I thought, now everyone is going to say that Seles came to Paris for free publicity.

The following day I met with a representative from the WTA Tour Players Association. At that point all the WTA knew was that I was considering a return. They had no idea that a comeback was in the works. We had to keep that confidential until the plans were firm. The last thing I wanted to do was make a big deal out of a return and then not come through. At the meeting, we discussed the changes in rules and regulations that had occurred over the last two years. We also talked about what I would want in terms of security if I came back to the tour.

I had hoped to meet with a representative from one of my sponsors to try to settle our differences out of court. In the end, their schedule didn't allow us to meet during my trip, and for almost a year and a half, we were in litigation. Now I have a new sponsor, Nike, and our relationship is strong and extremely positive.

I never went to watch the French Open: it would have been too painful to watch the third French Open I'd missed since the attack.

When I returned from Paris, Mark called. "We still on track?" he asked. I told him we were. "Okay, then I'm pretty certain your exhibition match will be at the end of July. I don't know what city, yet. I'm still working on getting a good arena."

The comeback was rolling forward like a train — picking up speed with each day, each week. And I was on board, ready for the ride of my life.

June 6, 1995, Press Release:

MONICA SELES RETURNS TO THE COURT AGAINST MARTINA NAVRATILOVA LIVE ON THE CBS SPORTS SHOW SATURDAY, JULY 29

Seles also to conduct a Clinic at Special Olympics World Games

Monica Seles, formerly the top-ranked women's tennis player in the world, returns to the court for the first time in more than two years when "The CBS Sports Show" presents her long-anticipated comeback against the legendary Martina Navratilova on Saturday, July 29. The announcement was made today by David Kenin, President, CBS Sports.

"We are ecstatic that CBS Sports will showcase Monica Seles' return to competitive tennis," Kenin said. "Her absence during the past twenty-six months has left the sports world without one of its brightest stars. The match, which features two illustrious champions, already registers as a victory for Seles — signifying a triumph of spirit in overcoming a harrowing incident."

Prior to the July 29 match, Seles will make her first public appearance at the Special Olympics World Games in New Haven, Connecticut, on July 8. She will conduct a clinic with the Special Olympians as part of the Special Olympics World Games tennis competition. No announcement has yet been made about the WTA Tour Events in which Seles will compete.

Seles, twenty-one, has not played competitive tennis since April 30, 1993, when she was stabbed during a match in Hamburg, Germany. At the time of her forced withdrawal from tennis, Seles had won seven of the previous eight Grand Slam tournaments she entered.

Navratilova, thirty-eight, the nine-times Wimbledon singles champion who again made it to the finals in 1994, retired from singles competition in November, 1994. She has captured eighteen Grand Slam titles and 167 singles titles, more overall championships than any other woman or man in tennis history. She holds records for the longest consecutive match-winning streak (seventy-four) and for consecutive doubles victories (109 with Pam Shriver). She will team with Steffi Graf in doubles competition later this month at Wimbledon.

CBS Sports' Tim Ryan and Mary Carillo will provide commentary for the best-of-three-sets exhibition match.

The Special Olympics World Games were held on July 8 in New Haven, Connecticut. While I was nervous about my first public appearance before the exhibition with Martina, I was also very excited. I'd worked with Special Olympians through the WTA Tour, and had been chairperson of the WTA Tour Special Olympics Committee in the past. There's always been a place in my mind and heart for the courage and achievements of the Special Olympians, so I let Tony Godsick and others worry about security, logistics, and all the rest, and focused on making sure that I could spend as much time as possible with the athletes.

The day couldn't have begun any better. Tony arranged for me to talk with Sonya Bell (the gymnast I'd presented the Arete Award to in Chicago). It was a great reunion — we talked and giggled for hours. And then it was time to enter the stadium for the Special Olympics World Games.

When I walked out, a young Olympian ran up and hugged me. He was wearing a T-shirt whose inscription welcomed me back to tennis.

I was very moved. Then I was greeted by Eunice Kennedy Shriver, founder of the Special Olympics, and various members of the Kennedy family thanked me for my participation in the event. The Kennedys talked to me about their tennis and family competitions, and Mrs. Shriver even asked me for a tennis lesson so that she could "beat my sons the next time we play." Of course, I obliged.

My father, Tony, and my publicist, Linda Dozoretz, accompanied me throughout the day. There were more than 300 press representatives from around the world following my every move — which was both flattering and nerve-racking. I spent the day handing out awards to many of the Special Olympics tennis players, and I tried to treat each one as if they'd just won a Grand Slam. There were even opportunities to play exhibitions with the athletes. I played doubles matches with some, and my father and I hit balls to others. I was amazed at the athletes' skills and the speed of their returns. Some even hit balls past me — which made their day.

I stayed in New Haven long after the schedule was over, because my father and I wanted to attend the next day's closing ceremonies. The whole experience was wonderful, and I was impressed by each of the athletes I met. When my own courage and determination was mentioned during the games I felt embarrassed; they couldn't compare with the strength and spirit I admired in the Special Olympians. A few weeks later I was named the "No Nonsense American Woman of the Month." I asked for my honorarium to be donated to the Special Olympics.

After the World Games I returned to Florida to continue training for my exhibition — an exhibition with sponsors and two players, but no stadium at that point. We had a hard time finding an arena. Most large venues are booked months in advance, and we needed one in three weeks. Finally, we booked the Atlantic City Convention Center.

As the days and weeks passed, I began to get really nervous. I was worried about playing before thousands in the stands and millions on nationwide television. What if I didn't play well? I spoke to Dr. May each week to work on controlling my emotions and fears.

There was another problem. Since Paris, I'd been running to lose weight. My knees began hurting two and a half weeks before Atlantic City. They got so bad, it was painful to walk. I flew out to Vail to see Dr. Steadman: the diagnosis was tendonitis. Dr. Steadman understood that it was unrealistic to tell me to rest. I only had two weeks until my comeback. "Just try to do a lot of inner thigh strengthening exercises, don't practice for as long on the court, and definitely stop running," he instructed. Both of us knew that even if I had to play on one leg, I'd compete in Atlantic City.

The day before the exhibition Mark McCormack came down on a private jet to fly my mother, father, and me to Atlantic City. Betsy was in Vail at the time, so she flew separately and met us there. When we got to Caesar's Palace, I didn't expect anyone to greet us; I just planned to check in, and then go to the convention center courts to practice. I couldn't have been more wrong.

The fun started the moment I stepped out of the car. A red carpet was rolled out from the hotel entrance to my feet. Then a costumed Caesar and bejeweled Cleopatra welcomed me to Atlantic City. Girls in sparkling outfits threw rose petals at my feet as I walked. There were armfuls of flowers and thousands of flashbulbs. Initially, I'd been worried about security. "What if he comes?" I'd asked Mark. "What if he tries again?" He promised that Caesar's would provide top-notch security. I trusted Mark so completely that I relaxed and enjoyed the attention at Caesar's.

After I'd settled into my room, Dad and I went out to practice. At the courts, a large group of reporters was waiting for me. They wanted to see how I was going to play after two years. I'd been practicing in private, so no one knew if I was playing well. I began to rally with a college student who had agreed to be my hitting partner. Being scrutinized during practice didn't help my nerves, but I played well anyway.

That night I went to dinner with Betsy and Mark, but I was too nervous to eat. Before I went up to my room, Betsy and I talked alone.

"This is going to be a tough night," Betsy said. "Try to get some sleep, stay calm, and think about having fun. The important thing is what you've gone through, and what you've overcome. So just do the best you can and get a great night's sleep."

Of course, I couldn't sleep. I watched television until 3:00 am and, when I finally dozed off, I had some strange dreams. I was walking out to the court for the exhibition, and I kept tripping. I never actually got on the court, because there were all these obstacles in front of me. I could see the net in the distance, but I just couldn't reach it. And I kept seeing all these strange faces that twisted into monsters.

Morning came fast and, before I knew it, it was time to go down to the courts and warm up. I hit for twenty minutes, then headed for the locker room to change for the match. My father walked beside me to give some last-minute advice. It was the advice of a dad, not a coach: "Monica, just go out there and have fun. It's time for you to do that."

Martina was in the locker room when I arrived. "You know, there are so many experiences in life, and you need to look at this as a positive one," she said as she took in my worried look. "Of course you're going to be nervous — I was so nervous when I played my last singles match before retirement, because I wanted to go out well. The only advice I can give you is don't try to live up to anybody else's expectations. You've worked hard and deserve this."

I really appreciated everything Martina had done for me — her support throughout my recovery and her kindness. Later, I'd give her back her bracelet. And I'd tell her that she was right: it had brought me luck.

Betsy came into the locker room. We sat down in a corner and talked. She told me that she was very proud of me, and that it took a lot of courage to be able to move on with my life. "Go out there and kick some butt," she told me with a smile. I hugged her and thanked her for all her support.

A cameraman from CBS poked his head into the room. "Ten seconds," he said. Then he started counting down as Martina and I walked toward the court: "9 . . . 8 . . . 7 . . ."

"Please, sir, stop counting. You're making me too nervous. Just tell me when I have to step onto the court."

Martina went onto the court first. She got a wonderful reception.

"Now," the cameraman said. I walked forward. My heart was pounding so hard that its beat filled my ears. I stepped onto the court and into an overwhelming sea of clapping and cheers. The spectators were on their feet, and their cries of support drowned out the beat of my heart. This is all for me, I thought in amazement. How can I show them how much it means? I waved to the fans, bowed and curtseyed to thank them all for being there, for wanting to watch me play again. I'm home, I thought as I walked out, I'm home.

You're okay, I told myself before Martina and I began to play. Go out there and just have fun. Those were the things Dr. May and I had worked on. Those were the things that helped me to calm my nerves and focus.

"Seles to serve," the chair umpire called into her microphone. Double fault. The first serve of my comeback, and I double faulted. I had to laugh. I was so nervous during the first game that when I threw the ball up to serve, I couldn't see it. My legs were numb. This is going to be a long afternoon and you're going to be in deep trouble and make a fool of yourself if you don't calm down, I thought. I held my serve and won the game.

I hit some great shots, and some really bad ones to tie us, 3 all, in the first set. I've got to concentrate, I thought as I looked into the stands at Betsy, Mark, Stephanie Tolleson, and my parents. They were smiling — thrilled to see me out on the court. I don't think they cared whether I won or lost. They just wanted me to overcome, move on, live again. Breathe, Monica, I told myself. It was a close set, but I took it, 6–3.

I broke Martina's serve the first game of the second set. After that, I began to feel more comfortable, almost as if I'd never left the game. Everything I hit was going in — especially my passing shots. Only when I reached 5–2 did I run into difficulty: I couldn't finish the game. I was serving and I couldn't seem to concentrate. Normally, if my serves go out they are maybe one foot from the T. But I was so nervous that I couldn't control my wrist, and one serve went all the way to the baseline. Martina looked over at me with an expression that said, What the heck was that?

I kept double faulting on match point. Three times I had the opportunity to end the match and I double faulted. On the fourth match point I hit such a weak serve that it barely cleared the net. The ball dropped, then bounced high to Martina's killer backhand. I'm in trouble now, I thought. She's going to attack it from high up and hit a slice. It's a hard shot to hit on a fast, low supreme court surface, but with Martina, I thought I didn't have a prayer. Martina made contact, but her return bounced out. I'd won the match!

I looked over to my parents and mouthed the words, "I've done it." Their faces beamed. I ran to the net to hug Martina.

"You're back, girl," Martina said with a smile. "There's no question in my mind, you're back."

I shook the chair umpire's hand and then raced over to my parents and kissed them. "Dad, we really made it through," I whispered in my father's ear. Then I hugged Betsy and Mark, Stephanie, and Sonya Bell, who'd come to support my return, and thanked them all. I was surrounded by family and friends from IMG, the WTA, and the press, all of whom gave me their love and support, and I just couldn't stop smiling.

44

After Atlantic City, nothing could have stopped me from returning to professional tennis. There was just one question — what would I be ranked? I assumed that I'd return at whatever number I'd fallen to during my two-year recovery. But that wouldn't be the case.

The full credit goes to Martina Navratilova. She's the one who developed the idea, and she's the one who held onto her beliefs, even when everyone else said it was the stupidest thing they'd ever heard. When our exhibition was announced, Martina, as President of the WTA Tour Players Association, suggested to the WTA and top players that if I came back to the tour, I should be ranked co-number one with Steffi Graf. The idea was met with strong opposition.

I never asked for special ranking consideration from the WTA and players if I returned to the tour. No special consideration had been given at the time of the attack, but after two years, I'd learned to accept that. The WTA's decision on rank wouldn't have affected my plans to return. However, they sent me a signed proposal about the co-number one ranking and I added my signature, thereby accepting the deal.

Unfortunately, the top players subsequently met at Wimbledon and stated that they did not agree with most of the elements of the proposal. There were weeks of meetings between the WTA Tour and the players but, in the end, the WTA Tour decided to honor the proposal. The decision surprised me and also made me even more determined to play well to show everyone that I'd only been given back my rightful place.

There was another factor in the WTA's decision: had they left me a wild card entry player, and a top-ranked player then faced me and lost in an early round, it would have been devastating to that player's ranking. Moreover, it would have eliminated a big tournament draw early in the event. The WTA knew from past experience that when I returned I'd be playing good tennis. They didn't want top players to face me as a wild card.

After the attack everyone thought they understood my life. They'd watched me grow up on court, seen me play countless tournaments, witnessed the stabbing on television — what more was there? From that one event they drew conclusions on my recuperation, my devotion to the game, my psyche. I read articles after the stabbing that said I was enjoying the "three-ring atmosphere" created by the attack; that I was staying out of the game to collect insurance (I didn't collect a dime), and to increase my chances of a substantial lawsuit against the German Tennis Federation.

I think various motives lay behind those articles: some members of the press wanted to minimize the attack and draw me back into the game. But the attack did happen and, at age nineteen, I had to deal with it. I'd never be the same, whether or not I returned to tennis. I had to accept that, and so did they.

Several reporters and commentators used the stabbing as a means to their own end — namely, to make a more controversial news story. Some of them even said that I was faking the severity of my injury and that I enjoyed the media circus. When I heard these comments, I was surprised and felt that it was quite wrong for professional reporters to say such prejudiced things.

Top ten players have no friends at their level on the tour. Friends tell each other secrets, share vulnerabilities, but you cannot show anyone on the tour your weaknesses: it would give your opponent a huge advantage over you, and there's no doubt she'll use it the next day on the court. I can't recall one top player relationship that turned into a real friendship spanning years. It just doesn't happen. Respect — that's possible.

Lower-ranked players tend to develop closer ties to each other, partly because they have to share rooms and rental cars to cut down the cost of their travel. They also play doubles matches together to make additional money.

The truth is that even if I had wanted to make close friends among the top players, there just isn't time. Let's say I'm playing the US Open and my match is at 1:00 pm. I get up in the morning, have breakfast and stretch. I get to the stadium by 11:00 am and practice for thirty minutes. Afterwards I go to the locker room to change. Now I need time to relax and focus. I put on my walkman and think about my match. Time to play. When I'm finished, I switch my wet shirt for a dry one and go into the press conference. Then I grab my things from the locker room and go home to rest. I want to spend time with my family, or the one or two friends I have outside of the game. Or, after playing before a packed stadium and meeting with the press, I just want to be alone. The last thing I'm going to do is hang out in the locker room and try to make friends.

The only occasions I've ever spent time with top players is at exhibition matches. Exhibitions are very enjoyable — there's less pressure, and the organizers try to plan dinners and day trips for the players. I've had a lot of fun at exhibitions with Jennifer Capriati, Martina Navratilova, and Gabriela Sabatini. Still, I think they would all say that the last thing they want to do at a major tournament is sit and chat with another top player. It isn't done, because it isn't smart tennis.

There are some things that will never hurt, and one of them is "Late Night with David Letterman." I've been a fan of Dave's for years, and even appeared on his show before the attack. During the two years following the stabbing, his staff had contacted me for an interview. Up until August 1995 I felt I had nothing to say. But after my exhibition with Martina I was finally ready to pay Dave a visit.

Tony Godsick arranged a pre-interview meeting so that one of Dave's producers could go over questions in advance. I decided that I wanted to be funny, so I made up my own ideas for a "Monica Top Ten List." I spent the day of the actual taping running my ideas by Tony. By the time we arrived at CBS for the show, I had enough material to host my own comedy show. But nothing could have prepared me for the reception I got when I entered the studio. The audience gave me a standing ovation, and Dave gave me a long, sentimental introduction. By the end of the interview, I felt as if I was back in the swing of life — and it was time to play some tennis.

Following the Atlantic City exhibition I had rejoined the tour. I was ready to get back in the game, despite my security concerns and my continued emotional ups and downs. I decided to play in the 1995 US Open at the end of August, and knew that I needed a professional match before that Grand Slam.

Unfortunately the tendonitis in my left knee had become worse since my exhibition, and there was nothing I could do but rest my leg. I finally decided that I'd be able to play in the Canadian Open in mid-August, but I didn't expect a great performance in Toronto. Even if I don't do well, it's important to play a professional match, I reminded myself.

Betsy Nagelsen was commentating on the Open for ESPN. It was great to have her there, not only for support, but to show me a city I'd never visited. In addition, I had a wonderful time with my fellow players. The first night of the tournament they held a welcome back party for me. It was great to see my generation, along with a new group of players I didn't know.

My first match on Tuesday, August 15, was against the American, Kimberly Po. It was a night match, which meant I had all day to get nervous. When I walked into the stadium with my bodyguards, the spectators rose in one wave and began to clap. As I'd never played in Toronto, I wasn't sure how the fans would react. Their support was more than I could have hoped for, but the match itself was uneventful: I took the first set, 6–0, and the second, 6–3.

By the day of my third round, I was feeling slightly less tense. I was scheduled to play Nathalie Tauziat from France. Nathalie and I had played countless matches in the past. During our last one, she'd complained repeatedly to the umpire about my grunts. Water under the bridge, I thought when I ran into her some hours before our round. It was the first time we'd seen each other in two years and I expected a "hello" from her, if not a "welcome back," but she walked past me without saying a word. Later that day I won, 6–2, 6–2. This time, there were no complaints about my grunting.

Despite the fact that I was nervous, I found myself enjoying my time in Toronto. Betsy, Tony, and my hitting partner for the tournament, Jimmy, and I even went to a VanHalen concert. We couldn't stay late because I had a match the next day, but we did hear an unforgettable drum solo. On the way back to the hotel, Jimmy admitted that he knew how to play the piano by ear. When we got to the hotel, we searched for a piano so that we could hear him play. The only one available was in the lounge. As Jimmy sat down, I silently hoped he really knew how to play because the lounge was full of people. He was great! As the songs flowed, the night took on a magical quality.

Reaching the quarterfinals of the Canadian Open was a shocker, since I'd had so little practice. Just go out there and have fun, I told myself before the match against Anke Huber of Germany. Anke is a strong back-court player. She doesn't miss a lot of balls, and we had a close match with some great points. When I won, 6–3, 6–2, no one was more surprised than me.

"I don't mind losing to someone like her," I said to Betsy with pre-game jitters before my semifinals match against Gabriela Sabatini. Betsy told me to think positively. I've always been a pessimist before a big match — even before the attack. As I walked out to the court, I thought how nice it was that some things never change.

The match against Gaby was only forty-eight minutes long. I won, 6–1, 6–0. I'd made it to the finals in my first professional match in two years!

After the Saturday semis Betsy and I went shopping for jewelry. I've never been good at making simple decisions: I can plan my professional tour schedule a year ahead, but that day I couldn't decide which little silver ring I wanted to buy. Betsy and I stood at the counter for over an hour.

When we'd first entered the store, a couple from America had been browsing beside us. They returned while I was still trying to decide which ring I wanted. "You know, Monica," they said, "we just realized it's taken you longer to pick out a silver ring than it took you to beat Sabatini!"

Amanda Coetzer from South Africa was my opponent in the finals of the Canadian Open. Amanda had upset Steffi Graf in the first round of the tournament. I'd played her before and had a hard time: she is a very steady player, she runs down every ball and doesn't make many errors. My father and I had a long talk before I walked onto center court. "This is a new beginning, Monica," Dad said. "You're playing great tennis. But most importantly, you're back in the game. Go out there and have a good time." I was still certain I was going to lose.

The match was over in only fifty-one minutes. I won, 6–0, 6–1. Later, Amanda would say that, "[Monica] just didn't allow me to play my game. She doesn't give you a lot of time. You have to get used to how fast the ball comes at you. You get to a point where you're confused. I wasn't sure what to do." When the match ended, I was dazed. I went over to my parents and hugged them. My father was crying.

"I can't believe this is for real. It's been such a long time and I was never sure I would ever play tennis again," I told the Canadian crowd at the awards ceremony. My father continued to cry as I thanked my family, friends, and fans. Then I fell silent as waves of applause rolled down from the stands. I thought about the two years it had taken me to reach that moment — about my fight to overcome personal demons, my father's battle against cancer, my mother's struggle to support her family. None of us were the same people we'd been twenty-eight months ago, on the morning I left to play a quarterfinals match in Hamburg. Now we truly understood the depth of our love, and the value of friends. No matter what happened at the US Open, I knew I'd already won.

Where was Betsy? She wasn't supposed to be commentating on my first match in the 1995 US Open for ESPN. She was supposed to be sitting with my family in our box beside the court. So where was she? I was playing my first-round match in the Grand Slam. My opponent was the Romanian, Ruxandra Dragomir. And I was nervous.

I was so tense that I showed up at the National Tennis Center in Flushing Meadows at 7:00 am, and my match wasn't until that night. I spent the day practicing and doing physical therapy. There were just too many hours to waste. I tried to eat, to nap, to watch television, but all I could do was pace and worry, worry and pace. By the time I got back to the tennis center, I was so tight that the muscles in my face ached. This was my first Grand Slam in two years. I'd worked so hard to get there . . . Oh boy, Monica, I thought. You'd better just calm down or you're not going to be able to see the ball.

But I could see the ball. What I couldn't see was my friend, Betsy. During the first set I scanned the stands: no Betsy. Her seat beside my parents was empty. Halfway through the match my eye caught a familiar face in Dragomir's box: it was Betsy! What the heck was she doing in the Romanian girl's box? The look on her face was comical. I turned back to the game and focused on taking the first set, 6–3. By the second set, I'd found my groove and began to hit winner after winner to take the set, 6–1. As I shook Ruxandra's hand, I realized that I'd never felt such a sense of accomplishment from a first-round win. I ran over to my parents.

My father was crying again. "You did it, Monica," he said as the tears streamed. I smiled and hugged him tight. Then I turned and hugged former New York Mayor, David Dinkins, who has been a friend and supporter throughout my recovery. Finally, I hugged my mother, who was also crying. Then I went to the locker room to change. On the way, I ran into Betsy.

"Boy, do I have a funny story to tell you," Betsy said with a grin. "I got the boxes confused. I thought I was in the right place, and then I looked across the court and saw your parents. I didn't want to miss any of the match by walking around the whole stadium, so I stayed. You should have seen the look on your face when you recognized me!" We both laughed about it while I changed and ran to the press conference.

"For a long time I mean I dreamed of this but I didn't envision it so just that for me right now is the main thing hopefully now it is just do your best and early next year it's going to be more going back to that really competitiveness and . . ." That's just a sample sentence from my press conference. I was so excited about winning the match that I forgot to take a breath as I talked to the media. If they minded, they didn't let on.

That night, Betsy and I went to a Manhattan restaurant for dinner. When I walked into the dining room, the whole restaurant started to clap. I'd never had such a nice reception in New York. The next day I went for a walk in Central Park. Wherever I went, people stopped to congratulate me on my comeback. Even a guy on roller blades sailed past and gave me a high five! I found myself enjoying Manhattan, just as I'd enjoyed Toronto. I went to two Broadway shows, made a presentation at the MTV Music Awards — even went to a Giants football game. Life felt fresh, new, and exciting. And I was having a ball.

As my rounds progressed, I continued to play pretty well — I wasn't playing great, but well enough to make it to a fourth-round match against Anke Huber. I knew it would be a tough one. The day was extremely hot, and the wind was swirling across the court. My father says that one of my worst faults is that I can't read the wind. After windy matches he asks me which way it was blowing, and I have no idea. That makes it hard to compensate.

Anke began the match by running me sideways and my left knee started to hurt as I raced across the court. It was already sore, and I'd been wearing a brace, taking anti-inflammatory pills, and working with my physical therapist. I knew I had to take control of the match, or my knee would just get worse. I took it in two sets, 6–1, 6–4.

In the quarterfinals I played Jana Novotna. She is a strong serve-and-volley player, and I'd lost to her in the past. That day I battled to take the first set and clinched it in a tie-breaker, 7–6. I won the second set fairly easily, 6–2, and proceeded to the semifinals in disbelief.

If anyone had told me I'd make it to the semis in my first Grand Slam since the attack, I wouldn't have believed them. I was still overweight, had a bad knee, and hadn't been able to practice consistently. Still, there I was playing Conchita Martinez from Spain.

Coming into our semis, Conchita hadn't lost a set. She had a great record, and had just won two hardcourt tournaments, which meant she was on a roll. Our match was held at 5:00 pm, which was unfortunate: it wouldn't be over until 7:30, and I wouldn't get back to the hotel until 8:30 that night. After dinner, it would be time to go to sleep. If I won the semis, I'd only have that night to recover before playing in the finals the following day. But that's what I had to do, because I won, 6–2, 6–2.

I had no time to think: I went home, ate, slept, woke, ate, stretched, warmed up, and then went to the National Tennis Center to play Steffi Graf in the finals of the US Open. Our match was everything the media and fans had hoped for: a showdown between the two number one players in the world.

When I got to the locker room to change, Steffi was already there. I said hello and then went to my locker to get ready. A few minutes later a tournament official called us and we walked down the tunnel together to center court. There was so much excitement in the stands. The spectators cheered and clapped for both of us, and hundreds of photographers snapped photos as we moved onto the court. I tried not to think about my history with Steffi — tried not to think about Parche, and how he'd stabbed me for the woman across the court, stabbed me to make her number one . . . But now I was co-number one. Concentrate, Monica, I instructed. And then the match began.

It was so close. We fought for each point, each game. We held our serves until we reached 6 all in the first set: tie-breaker. You can do this, I told myself as I served. And I could, and I did, until I was up, 6–5, with a chance to serve for the first set. I tossed the ball and hit it hard down the middle. Steffi lunged for the line, but missed her shot. I pumped my fist over my head in victory: I thought I'd taken the first set. But the umpire overruled the linesman.

"Serve was wide," he said in a late call.

Wide? It wasn't wide, it was right on the line. I went over to the umpire and argued the point. He wouldn't budge, so I went back in frustration and hit a second serve. Steffi returned it with a beautiful forehand to bring us to 6 all. I missed the next point and Steffi won the tie-breaker and the first set. I was crushed.

It's not like me to hang on to a point. When it's over, I move on. But I couldn't move on to that second set. From my point of view the call had been unfair (I believe that to this day), and I just couldn't let it go. I took the second set, 6–0, but it didn't feel like I'd won it easily. Throughout the set, I replayed that tie-breaker serve. I was still mad when we began the third set.

The crowd finally began to change my mood. They were cheering so loud that I realized they thought I might actually win the match. I hadn't even considered that. It was my first Grand Slam in two and a half years — I was thrilled to get to the finals. But win it? I served an ace at 2 games apiece. The umpire called it out. It was just one of many calls I felt he made against me that match. In fact there wasn't one close call he gave me. I felt my anger grow again. Steffi broke me and took the lead, 3–2. After that, I couldn't seem to concentrate. I felt my game slipping and there was nothing I could do. Steffi took the set, 6–3, and won the match and the 1995 US Open title.

I walked to the net to congratulate my opponent. But instead of coming forward to shake my hand, Steffi ran over to her box and hugged her mother. It was a strange thing to do to another player — and I don't recall it ever happening in tennis before. The respectful procedure is to shake your opponent's hand and then go to your family and friends, not vice versa. I stood at the net wondering what I should do. Finally Steffi returned and we shook hands and kissed on the cheeks. Then I went over to my parents and thanked them for being so supportive of me. I would have liked my comeback Grand Slam to have had a happy ending, but I was still pleased to have played in the finals.

Later, I would learn that Steffi called our finals match the biggest win of her life. That interpretation of our match was incomprehensible to me, and to a lot of other people. But the most important thing was that I was back in the game. If there was any doubt in the top players' minds that I didn't deserve to be ranked co-number one, I think it was gone. And from the cheers and applause at the Canadian and US Open, I knew that the fans appreciated my comeback and my game.

$$\left(48\right)$$

Some players only sign autographs if they win a match. I sign, win or lose. In 1992 I spent almost two hours signing on the court after I won the Virginia Slims Championship. You can never be as happy when you lose as you are when you win, but when I sign after a loss, the appreciation I get helps to make up for it. I look into those kids' eyes and see myself just a few years ago, asking Martina and Chris for a signature. How excited I was when they signed!

Not all athletes are gracious to their fans. I still recall asking a Chinese ping-pong player for his autograph at the World Championships, and being told to buzz off. So today I stay until every last kid has my signature on T-shirt, tennis balls, sneakers or baseball cap.

When I was a junior player I asked John McEnroe to pose for a photograph.

"Sure," Mr. McEnroe replied as we stood in a hotel lobby.

I have the photograph to this day. Ten, maybe fifteen seconds — that's all it took John to make my day and give me a memory that I'd cherish for a lifetime. I think it's not too much to ask. It's nothing in return for what the fans give me — for their cheers and applause. And since the attack, it's the least I can do for all their love and support.

Before the attack I received a lot of fan mail. People wrote to tell me that they liked to watch me play, or that they wanted to be tennis stars.

Dear Monica,
I'm nine years old. I look up to you. I want to be like you and hit

the ball with two hands on my racket. I want to grunt like you. I love you.
Scott

After the attack the letters changed. Even the children understood what had happened and wanted to help.

Dear Monica,
Please don't hate me because I'm German. I'm so sorry. If you ever come back to my country, I'll protect you.
Love,
Barbara (age eight)

Fans started opening up to me. Young women who'd been attacked or raped wrote empathetic letters, shared their stories, gave advice. Parents began calling my agent to ask me to talk to their children to try to get them out of trouble, or help them cope with a debilitating illness or handicap. All of a sudden I was a human being whom people could relate to, share their problems with, give support to and ask for help. I'd always tried to give something back to my fans by signing autographs, sending photographs, and doing charity work. After the attack, I was in a position to do more than that.

Dear Monica,
My son is eleven years old and suffering from leukemia. He refuses to take his medication, and I'm afraid if he doesn't continue his treatment, he'll die. Would you please call and try to talk to him?
I know it's a lot to ask, but I don't know where else to turn . . .

It's amazing how children will listen to me when I tell them to take their medicine. But that's happened on countless occasions and it felt so good to help. I visited kids in hospitals to cheer them up. I remember a little girl in Houston who was a great tennis player, but lost her arm in an accident. She didn't want to attend physical therapy. I talked to her about how important it was, and told her that she'd be able to play tennis again if she worked really hard. I tried to explain that it didn't matter whether or not she won matches, just that she loved the game. "That's why I play," I said. The little girl started going to therapy.

There was the call from a distraught mother whose daughter had fallen down on the field unconscious during soccer practice and awoke to find her entire left side paralyzed. I telephoned the girl and we talked about the problems we shared — how it was hard to face each morning.

It's nice that people now see me as a human being who can empathize with their lives, their children. Maybe it's because I'm young that the kids can relate to me; maybe it's because I'm an athlete; or perhaps it's simply because I care. It's only in the aftermath of the stabbing that I've understood completely that my fans aren't just there for me. I'm there for them, too.

Over the past few years I've come to realize that tennis is only my first career. Long after it's over, I know I'll be working with children, helping them through difficult situations and disabilities. And maybe I'll be lucky enough to make them feel as good as my fans, young and old, have made me feel.

49

I lost in the finals of the 1995 US Open against Steffi Graf, but I played well enough to dispel any doubts about my comeback in my competitors' minds. Still, I felt I had more to prove. With that in mind, I flew to Sydney in early January of 1996 to play in the Peters NSW Open. I'd decided to add that competition before the Australian Open, which meant I'd play three major tournaments in a row in a span of one month — the Peters, the Australian Open, and Tokyo. After spending the fall of 1995 nursing ankle and knee injuries, it was an ambitious schedule.

I had a week before the tournament began, which was lucky because the time change had left me exhausted. The second day I broke my racket because I was so tired I just let it fall out of my hand. Each morning I went to practice from 7:00 am to 9:00 am — and by 7:15 it started raining. I didn't get to practice as much as I wanted, but it was still enough. After practice, the media would begin to follow me around. That took a little while to get used to, but my appearance in Australia was news, and the press were really nice so I didn't mind.

A few days before the tournament began, I did some sightseeing — visited the Opera House, went on a water cruise, swam at Bondai Beach. I had fun, and I relaxed, and by the time my first match began, I felt healthy, uninjured, and ready to play.

During the Peters NSW Open I played every single big hitter in Australia. Still, I made it to the quarterfinals against Mariaan De Swardt from South Africa. Mariaan is the second hardest server in women's tennis, and we battled harder than the score reflected (6–3, 6–2). In the semis I faced Brenda Schultz-McCarthy, the biggest server. I've played her in the past, and when her first serve goes in — watch out! That day Brenda was playing some great tennis: I fought to take the first set in a tie-breaker, 7–6 (7–4), and was relieved to win the second, 6–3. I'd made it to the finals.

I had never played American Lindsay Davenport before the finals of the Peters NSW Open, and I didn't know what to expect. What I didn't expect was to lose the first set, 4–6. Lindsay played great all-round tennis, and I had to tell myself to focus to get back into the game. I took the next set in a tie-breaker, 7–6 (9–7), and the third, 6–3. I had won the Peters Open, but not without paying a price. During my match with Lindsay I pulled a groin muscle. It wasn't any one shot or lunge that did it — it was the fact that Rebound Ace courts are a bit stickier than I'm used to.

There was no time to worry about my injury. After the awards ceremony IMG representative Tony Godsick, my father and I raced to our car. Our flight to Melbourne was leaving in fifteen minutes, and the ride to the airport usually took twenty-five. I had to get to Melbourne that night, otherwise I wouldn't even have one day to prepare for the Australian Open. Thank goodness the Sydney police understood: as we piled into our minivan, an unmarked police car with a "Kojak" siren on top pulled out in front of us. A marked police car with more sirens pulled behind us, and we raced off to the airport. I wish I'd had a video camera — it was just like the movies! We made our flight with minutes to spare and headed off, exhausted but happy, to Melbourne.

I arrived in Melbourne late on Sunday night, and only had time to unpack before falling into bed. On Monday morning I woke early to practice, then went to get some physical therapy for my groin muscle. I was worried by the fact that I didn't have more than one day to relax and to get used to the Australian Open courts before playing on Tuesday, but there was nothing I could do.

My early rounds went fairly easily. I was still feeling strong and, while my groin hurt, it was bearable. In the quarterfinals I faced Iva Majoli from Croatia in a quick match, 6–1, 6–2. I had the following day off, so I planned to go to a movie with Betsy Nagelsen, who was there commentating on the tournament. That day, Arantxa Sanchez Vicario was playing her quarterfinals match against an American, Chanda Rubin. Since I'd never seen Chanda play, and would play the winner of their match in the semifinals, I turned on the television just before going out to meet Betsy. I watched for a few moments, then left. When I returned to my hotel room three hours later, I flicked on the television: Arantxa and Chanda were still playing. A score flashed — 12–12. This has got to be a rerun, I thought. Just to make sure, I called Tony. He told me that the match was live — it had been going on for more than three hours. I watched as Arantxa and Chanda battled for the third set, with Chanda taking it, 16–14, to win the quarterfinals in the second longest women's match in history at three hours and thirty-three minutes. It was one of the best matches ever in women's tennis. Oh boy, I thought excitedly, I'm going to play that girl in the semifinals.

At practice the next morning I started to serve and found that I couldn't lift my left arm above shoulder height. Every time I tried to serve, shooting pains ran around the joint and down my arm. What was going on? My father and I left the court and began a regimen of hourly icing and massage therapy. I took some pain pills, but nothing seemed to work. That night my physical therapist said that I had muscle strain or tendonitis in my shoulder. I'd have to endure the pain in the semifinals match until my shoulder warmed up. After that, I'd be all right. I went to bed that night wondering if I'd even be able to serve.

The first four games against Chanda Rubin were very painful. I tried not to show it as I swung and served because I didn't want her to see my weakness. But in my mind I was screaming, "Get me out of here, why am I doing this?" Chanda is a tough all-round player, and she is able to hit forehand winners from anywhere on the court. In the first set she did just that, taking me 6–7 (7–2).

I am not going to lose in the semifinals, I told myself. It wasn't just that I had something to prove to myself; everyone in Australia expected me to win the Open. I'd won it three consecutive years, 1991–93, and only the attack in Hamburg had kept me from trying to win more consecutive Australian Opens than anyone else in the history of women's tennis. When I arrived in Melbourne, the media kept saying that I was going to win the Open and, in my mind, that meant I *had* to win it; there was no other option. It didn't matter that I'd barely played in two and a half years . . . I had to win. Get back in the game, Monica, I told myself after losing the first set. And I did.

I took the second set, 6–1. The soreness in my shoulder was still there, but I refused to let it stop me from serving. Then came the battle for the third set. I fought as hard as I could, but Chanda ruled the court until I trailed her 5–2. Come on, Monica, I murmured. I won my serve and brought us to 5–3, but then Chanda had the chance to serve for the match. However, she double-faulted, drove a volley wide, and ultimately I broke her serve to bring us to 5–5. After that, nothing could stop me. I took the next two games and won the match with a forehand down the line. I felt elation, relief, and a dull ache in my shoulder as I walked to the net to shake Chanda's hand.

No one had said that the Australian Open was going to be easy, but when Anke Huber broke my serve in the first set of the finals and took a 3–2 lead, I knew that she was on and I was in for a tough day. Anke is a very high-paced player and I had to match her pace with hard, deep ground strokes. I took the first set, 6–4, and then soared through the second, 6–1.

And then I was on center court with a Grand Slam trophy in my hands, standing before a crowd of cheering fans; hugging my father, mother, Mark McCormack and Betsy; feeling as if it was 1994, not 1996 — as if those two and a half years of exile had never happened, as if I'd never been out of the game and this was my fourth consecutive Australian Open win, not just my fourth . . .

I went to the locker room to change into a dry shirt and go to my press conference. I don't remember walking: I floated along on a sea of applause, of smiles, of exhilaration. I entered the conference feeling confident, happy, at peace. The press started clapping when they saw me, and then they began to ask questions. "What was it like to win my first Grand Slam title as an American?" I told them I'd felt like an American for many years now, but that it still felt incredible. "Tell us about your injuries; are they bad?" My shoulder, I explained, was quite sore, but I felt with physical therapy it would heal quickly. "Do you think Jennifer Capriati will return to tennis?" That's up to her, I said, but I hope she will.

"Will you play a tournament in Germany again?" a male reporter called out. I took a deep breath before I answered that one. "Ms. Seles, will you play in a tournament in Germany again?" the reporter repeated.

"I don't know," I said. "For me, what's very hard, and if you were in my position it would be very hard, is to go where this happened in front of thousands of people and the person who did it was not put in jail for a day. I think that it's very hard to go back and feel safe again."*

"Don't you think it would complete your recovery to go back to Germany?" the reporter pressed.

"I don't know . . . I mean, whatever happened there has not been fair. But I don't want to think about that," I said. And then it hit me. For a few minutes I'd felt like the nightmare of the last few years hadn't happened. I had just won a Grand Slam — the first since my return — and stood before thousands with a trophy held high over my head and listened to their support, their appreciation for my game. All I wanted to do was to enjoy this day without thinking about the past. But that reporter refused to let me have that. I felt the tears well up in my eyes and pulled my baseball cap down to hide them as they coursed down my cheeks. I heard the cameras clicking furiously. "Please don't take photographs of this," I asked softly.

* A few weeks later Billy Jean King, Federation Cup Captain, made a statement to the press that the United States team would object to playing the Federation Cup in Germany. "We should definitely have a neutral place," she explained.

"Monica, do you have any fun plans while you're in Melbourne?" a kind reporter asked.

I tried to answer, tried to swallow the frustration and sadness, but I couldn't. "There's no point in continuing with this," I said when I realized that I just couldn't compose myself. I rose and left. It was the second time in a row that a Grand Slam winner had walked out of her press conference. At the US Open Steffi had been reduced to tears and left the conference room after questions about her father.

"Don't worry about them," Tony Godsick soothed as I cried in the hallway. I went back to the locker room and Betsy, my mother, Mary Joe Fernandez and Edwina (an Australian friend) joined me. I continued to cry. "Why couldn't he just let me be happy?" I asked. No one had any answers. I wanted to go back to the conference and explain that I didn't blame Germany or the German people for Parche's actions. That someday I do hope to conquer my fears and play in that beautiful country where I still have many friends. But I was too upset to talk to anyone. Instead, I left the arena and went back to my hotel. I forgot my trophy.

That evening things got better. There's a Melbourne band called Young Elders who wrote a song a few years ago about me. Tony arranged for us to visit the band in their recording studio. They sang their song, "Fly Monica, Fly," to me, and even gave me a drum lesson. I returned home for some physical therapy and then went to a big dinner organized by Nike. That night Tony, Anke Huber, Mary Joe Fernandez and I went out to a dance club. I forgot about my upset and just enjoyed the music. It felt great to relax and have a good time with friends only hours after we'd battled on the court.

Nothing is ever like you think it's going to be. If I've learned anything over the past few years, that's it. Winning the Australian Open, my first Grand Slam since my return, was truly important to me — but not for the reasons I'd thought. Originally, I wanted to win to prove something to myself. Then, when the press kept reporting that I was going to win, I wanted to win to prove them right. But in the end it was about going onto a court and playing great tennis. That's what I missed most when my world was more darkness than light, and I realize now that it's not something anyone can take away from me.

MONICA SELES'S TENNIS CAREER

March 1988 — February 1996

1988

March

VIRGINIA SLIMS OF FLORIDA, *Boca Raton*

Outdoor/Hard   Draw: 64   Rank: S000

R64   w   Kelesi, Helen   7–6 (7–3) 6–3
R32   L   Evert, Chris   6–2   6–1

March

LIPTON INTERNATIONAL PLAYERS' CHAMPIONSHIPS, *Key Biscayne*

Outdoor/Hard   Draw: 128   Rank: S000

R128 w   Field, Louise   6–0   6–3
R64   L   Sabatini, Gabriela   7–6   6–3

October

VIRGINIA SLIMS OF NEW ORLEANS, *New Orleans*

Outdoor/Hard   Draw: 32   Rank: S000

R32	W	Frazier, Amy	4–6	6–4	7–6 (7–1)
R16	W	Magers, Gretchen	6–4	6–4	
Q	W	McNeil, Lori	6–1	6–3	
S	L	Smith, Anne	6–1	4–3	Ret

1989

February

VIRGINIA SLIMS OF WASHINGTON, *Washington*

Indoor/Carpet   Draw: 32   Rank: S085

R32	W	Savchenko, Larisa	6–0	6–2
R16	W	White, Robin	6–3	6–0
Q	W	Maleeva, Manuela	6–2	6–4
S	L	Garrison, Zina	Def	

April

VIRGINIA SLIMS OF HOUSTON, *Houston*

Outdoor/Clay   Draw: 32   Rank: S000

R32	W	Daniels, Mary Lou	6–2	6–3	
R16	W	Frazier, Amy	5–7	6–4	6–2
Q	W	Temesvari, Andrea	6–2	7–5	

S	W	Cunningham, Carrie	6–0	6–1	
F	W	Evert, Chris	3–6	6–1	6–4

June

FRENCH OPEN, *Paris*

Outdoor/Clay Draw: 128 Rank: S022

R128	W	Reis, Ronni	6–4	6–1	
R64	W	Martin, Stacey	6–0	6–2	
R32	W	Garrison, Zina	6–3	6–2	
R16	W	Faull, Jo-Anne	6–3	6–2	
Q	W	Maleeva, Manuela	6–3	7–5	
S	L	Graf, Steffi	6–3	3–6	6–3

July

WIMBLEDON, *London*

Outdoor/Grass Draw: 128 Rank: S013 Seed: 11

R128	W	Schultz, Brenda	7–6 (7–3)	1–6	6–4
R64	W	Porwik, Claudia	6–2	6–4	
R32	W	Sviglerova, Eva	6–4	6–3	
R16	L	Graf, Steffi	6–0	6–1	

September

US OPEN, *New York*

Outdoor/Hard   Draw: 128   Rank: S012   Seed: 12

R128	W	Henricksson, Ann	4–6	6–2	6–2
R64	W	Smith, Anne	7–5	6–2	
R32	W	Stafford, Shaun	7–6 (7–3)	6–2	
R16	L	Evert, Chris	6–0	6–2	

September

VIRGINIA SLIMS OF DALLAS, *Dallas*

Indoor/Carpet   Draw: 32   Rank: S010   Seed: 5

R32	W	Bunge, Bettina	6–7 (0–7)	6–4	6–0
R16	W	Burgin, Elise	6–2	6–3	
Q	W	Sanchez, Arantxa	6–4	6–2	
S	W	Smith, Anne	6–1	6–2	
F	L	Navratilova, Martina	7–6 (7–2)	6–3	

October

PORSCHE TENNIS GRAND PRIX, *Filderstad*

Indoor/Carpet   Draw: 32   Rank: S009   Seed: 4

R32	W	Schultz, Brenda	4–6	6–3	6–4
R16	W	Hanika, Sylvia	6–3	6–4	
Q	L	Fernandez, Mary Joe	6–4	4–6	7–6

October

EUROPEAN INDOORS, *Zurich*

Indoor/Carpet   Draw: 32   Rank: S009   Seed: 4

R32	W	Zardo, Emanuela	6–1	6–2
R16	W	McNeil, Lori	7–6 (7–5)	6–2
Q	W	Kelesi, Helen	6–0	6–0
S	L	Novotna, Jana	7–6	6–4

October

BRIGHTON INTERNATIONAL, *Brighton*

Indoor/Carpet   Draw: 32   Rank: S007   Seed: 3

R32	W	Herreman, Nathalie	6–3	6–4
R16	W	Henricksson, Ann	6–3	6–1
Q	W	Mandlikova, Hana	6–0	6–1
S	W	Maleeva, Manuela	6–3	6–2
F	L	Graf, Steffi	7–5	6–4

November

VIRGINIA SLIMS CHAMPIONSHIPS, *New York*

Indoor/Carpet   Draw: 16   Seed: 6

| R16 | W | Martinez, Conchita | 6–0 | 6–1 | |
| Q | L | Navratilova, Martina | 6–3 | 5–7 | 7–5 |

1990

February

VIRGINIA SLIMS OF CHICAGO, *Chicago*

Indoor/Carpet   Draw: 32   Rank: S006   Seed: 4

R32   L   Fairbank-Nideffe,
            Rosalyn   6–3   6–4

February

VIRGINIA SLIMS OF WASHINGTON, *Washington*

Indoor/Carpet   Draw: 32   Rank: S006   Seed: 3

R32   W   Bye, Bye
R16   W   Martin, Stacey   Def
Q   W   Shriver, Pam   6–2   7–6 (7–5)
S   L   Navratilova, Martina 6–3   6–0

March

VIRGINIA SLIMS OF FLORIDA, *Boca Raton*

Ourdoor/Hard   Draw: 64   Rank: S006   Seed: 2

R64   W   Bye, Bye
R32   W   Jagerman, Nicole   6–2   6–0
R16   L   Gildemeister, Laura 6–1   7–5

March

LIPTON PLAYERS' CHAMPIONSHIPS, *Key Biscayne*

Outdoor/Hard · · · · · · · Draw: 128 · · · · · · · Rank: S006 · · · · · · · Seed: 3

R128	W	Bye, Bye		
R64	W	Harvey-Wild, Linda	6–1	6–4
R32	W	Lapi, Laura	6–1	6–1
R16	W	Fairbank-Nideffer,		
		Rosalyn	6–3	6–4
Q	W	Herreman, Nathalie	6–3	6–1
S	W	Tauziat, Nathalie	6–3	6–1
F	W	Wiesner, Judith	6–1	6–2

March–April

US WOMEN'S HARDCOURT CHAMPIONSHIP, *San Antonio*

Outdoor/Hard · · · · · · · Draw: 16 · · · · · · · Rank: S004 · · · · · · · Seed: 2

R16	W	Smith, Anne	6–3	7–5
Q	W	Mandlikova, Hana	6–4	6–4
S	W	Fairbank-Nideffer,		
		Rosalyn	6–3	6–0
F	W	Maleeva, Manuela	6–4	6–3

April

ECKERD OPEN, *Tampa*

Outdoor/Clay · · · · · · · Draw: 32 · · · · · · · Rank: S003 · · · · · · · Seed: 1

R32	W	Collins, Sandy	6–1	6–1
R16	W	Faber, Donna	6–0	6–1

Q	W	Sloane, Susan	6–2	6–0
S	W	Martinez, Conchita	6–4	6–0
F	W	Maleeva, Katerina	6–1	6–0

May

ITALIAN OPEN, *Rome*

Outdoor/Clay   Draw: 64   Rank: S004   Seed: 2

R64	W	Bye, Bye		
R32	W	Zrubakova, Radka	6–4	6–1
R16	W	Paz, Mercedes	6–1	6–1
Q	W	Maleeva, Manuela	6–0	6–2
S	W	Kelesi, Helen	6–1	6–2
F	W	Navratilova, Martina	6–1	6–1

May

LUFTHANSA CUP, *Berlin*

Outdoor/Clay   Draw: 64   Rank: S003   Seed: 2

R64	W	Bye, Bye		
R32	W	Jagerman, Nicole	6–1	6–0
R16	W	Maleeva, Magdalena	6–2	6–3
Q	W	Martinez, Conchita	6–0	6–3
S	W	Cecchini, Sandra	6–1	6–3
F	W	Graf, Steffi	6–4	6–3

June

FRENCH OPEN, *Paris*

Outdoor/Clay		Draw: 128		Rank: S003		Seed: 2
R128	W	Piccolini, Katia	6–0	6–0	
R64	W	Kelesi, Helen	4–6	6–4	6–4
R32	W	Meskhi, Leila	7–6 (7–4)	7–6 (7–4)	
R16	W	Gildemeister, Laura	6–4	6–0	
Q	W	Maleeva, Manuela	3–6	6–1	7–5
S	W	Capriati, Jennifer	6–2	6–2	
F	W	Graf, Steffi	7–6	6–4	

July

WIMBLEDON, *London*

Outdoor/Grass		Draw: 128		Rank: S003		Seed: 3
R128	W	Strandlund, Maria	6–2	6–0	
R64	W	Benjamin, Camille	6–3	7–5	
R32	W	Minter, Anne	6–3	6–3	
R16	W	Henricksson, Ann	6–1	6–0	
Q	L	Garrison, Zina	3–6	6–3	9–7

August

VIRGINIA SLIMS OF LOS ANGELES, *Manhattan Beach*

Outdoor/Hard		Draw: 64		Rank: S003		Seed: 2
R64	W	Bye, Bye			
R32	W	Keller, Audra	6–2	6–2	

R16	W	Smith, Anne	6–3	6–3	
Q	W	Frazier, Amy	2–6	6–2	7–5
S	W	Fernandez, Mary Joe	6–1	6–0	
F	W	Navratilova, Martina	6–4	3–6	7–6 (8–6)

September

US OPEN, *New York*

Outdoor/Hard		Draw: 128	Rank: S003		Seed: 3

R128	W	Pampoulova, Elena	6–0	6–0	
R64	W	Fairbank-Nideffer,			
		Rosalyn	6–2	6–2	
R32	L	Ferrando, Linda	1–6	6–1	7–6 (7–3)

September

NICHIREI INTERNATIONAL, *Tokyo*

Indoor/Carpet		Draw: 32	Rank: S003		Seed: 2

R32	W	Bye, Bye			
R16	W	Pfaff, Eva	6–1	6–0	
Q	L	Frazier, Amy	5–7	7–5	6–2

October–November

VIRGINIA SLIMS OF CALIFORNIA, *Oakland*

Indoor/Carpet   Draw: 32   Rank: S003   Seed: 2

R32	W	Bye, Bye			
R16	W	Temesvari, Andrea	6–1	6–2	
Q	W	Rehe, Stephanie	6–1	6–2	
S	W	Garrison, Zina	6–1	3–6	6–2
F	W	Navratilova, Martina	6–3	7–6 (7–5)	

November

VIRGINIA SLIMS CHAMPIONSHIPS, *New York*

Indoor/Carpet   Draw: 16   Rank: S003   Seed: 2

R16	W	Paulus, Barbara	6–2	6–2			
Q	W	Sanchez Vicario, Arantxa	5–7	7–6	6–4		
S	W	Fernandez, Mary Joe	6–3	6–4			
F	W	Sabatini, Gabriela	6–4	5–7	3–6	6–4	6–2

1991

January

AUSTRALIAN OPEN, *Melbourne*

Outdoor/Hard   Draw: 128   Rank: S002   Seed: 2

R128	W	Hack, Sabine	6–0	6–0
R64	W	Caverzasio, Cathy	6–1	6–0

R32	w	Kschwendt, Karin	6–3	6–1	
R16	w	Tanvier, Catherine	6–2	6–1	
Q	w	Huber, Anke	6–3	6–1	
S	w	Fernandez, Mary Joe	6–3	0–6	9–7
F	w	Novotna, Jana	5–7	6–3	6–1

February–March

VIRGINIA SLIMS OF PALM SPRINGS, *Palm Springs*

Outdoor/Hard   Draw: 64   Rank: S002   Seed: 1

R64	w	Bye, Bye			
R32	w	Javer, Monique	6–3	6–1	
R16	w	Appelmans, Sabine	6–3	6–0	
Q	w	Hy, Patricia	7–5	6–2	
S	w	Kelesi, Helen	6–0	6–3	
F	L	Navratilova, Martina	6-2	7–6 (8–6)	

March

LIPTON INTERNATIONAL PLAYERS' CHAMPIONSHIPS, *Key Biscayne*

Outdoor/Hard   Draw: 128   Rank: S001   Seed: 2

R128	w	Bye, Bye			
R64	w	Cioffi, Halle	6–1	6–3	
R32	w	Kschwendt, Karin	6–0	6–1	
R16	w	Labat, Florencia	7–5	6–0	
Q	w	Capriati, Jennifer	2–6	6–1	6–4
S	w	Fernandez, Mary Joe	6–1	6–3	
F	w	Sabatini, Gabriela	6–3	7–5	

March

US WOMEN'S HARDCOURT CHAMPIONSHIPS, *San Antonio*

Outdoor/Hard   Draw: 32   Rank: S001   Seed: 1

R32	W	Labat, Florencia	6–0	6–1	
R16	W	Porwik, Claudia	6–1	6–4	
Q	W	De Lone, Erika	6–2	6–0	
S	W	Maleeva-Fragnier, Manuela	6–2	2–6	6–2
F	L	Graf, Steffi	6–4	6–3	

April

VIRGINIA SLIMS OF HOUSTON, *Houston*

Outdoor/Clay   Draw: 32   Rank: S001   Seed: 1

R32	W	Bye, Bye		
R16	W	Zrubakova, Radka	6–0	6–2
Q	W	Bonsignori, Federica	6–1	6–0
S	W	Cecchini, Sandra	6–0	6–2
F	W	Fernandez, Mary Joe	6–4	6–3

April–May

CITIZEN CUP, *Hamburg*

Outdoor/Clay   Draw: 64   Rank: S001   Seed: 1

R64	W	Bye, Bye		
R32	W	Leand, Andrea	6–1	6–1
R16	W	Rajchrtova, Regina	6–3	6–0

Q	W	Sukova, Helena	6–0	6–1	
S	W	Sanchez Vicario,			
		Arantxa	6–2	6–4	
F	L	Graf, Steffi	7–5	6–7 (4–7)	6–3

May

ITALIAN OPEN, *Rome*

Outdoor/Clay   Draw: 64   Rank: S001   Seed: 1

R64	W	Bye, Bye			
R32	W	Provis, Nicole	6–3	6–1	
R16	W	Piccolini, Katia	6–3	6–1	
Q	W	Meskhi, Leila	6–0	6–1	
S	W	Fernandez, Mary Joe	7–5	2–6	6–4
F	L	Sabatini, Gabriela	6–3	6–2	

June

FRENCH OPEN, *Paris*

Outdoor/Clay   Draw: 128   Rank: S001   Seed: 1

R128	W	Zrubakova, Radka	6–3	6–0	
R64	W	De Swardt, Mariaan	6–0	6–2	
R32	W	Quentrec, Karine	6–1	6–2	
R16	W	Cecchini, Sandra	3–6	6–3	6–0
Q	W	Martinez, Conchita	6–0	7–5	
S	W	Sabatini, Gabriela	6–4	6–1	
F	W	Sanchez Vicario,			
		Arantxa	6–3	6–4	

July–August

TENNIS CLASSIC, *San Diego*

Outdoor/Hard   Draw: 32   Rank: S001   Seed: 1

R32	W	Bye, Bye		
R16	W	Shriver, Pam	6–2	6–2
Q	W	Minter, Anne	6–0	6–3
S	W	Tauziat, Nathalie	6–1	6–2
F	L	Capriati, Jennifer	4–6	6–1	7–6 (7–2)

August

VIRGINIA SLIMS OF LOS ANGELES, *Manhattan Beach*

Outdoor/Hard   Draw: 64   Rank: S001   Seed: 1

R64	W	Bye, Bye		
R32	W	Reinach, Elna	6–1	6–0
R16	W	Coetzer, Amanda	6–4	6–1
Q	W	Paz, Mercedes	6–2	6–2
S	W	Sanchez Vicario, Arantxa	6–7 (5–7)	6–4	6–4
F	W	Date, Kimiko	6–3	6–1

August–September

US OPEN, *New York*

Outdoor/Hard   Draw: 128   Rank: S002   Seed: 1

R128	W	Arendt, Nicole	6–2	6–0
R64	W	Zardo, Emanuela	6–0	4–6	6–0

R32	w	Gomer, Sara	6–1	6–4	
R16	w	Rajchrtova, Regina	6–1	6–1	
Q	w	Fernandez, Gigi	6–1	6–2	
S	w	Capriati, Jennifer	6–3	3–6	7–6 (7–3)
F	w	Navratilova, Martina	7–6 (7–1)	6–1	

September

NICHIREI INTERNATIONAL, *Tokyo*

Outdoor/Hard   Draw: 32   Rank: S001   Seed: 1

R32	w	Bye, Bye		
R16	w	Hiraki, Rika	6–3	6–4
Q	w	Kidowaki, Maya	6–0	6–0
S	w	Frazier, Amy	6–4	6–0
F	w	Fernandez, Mary Joe	6–1	6–1

September–October

MILANO INDOOR, *Milan*

Indoor/Carpet   Draw: 32   Rank: S001   Seed: 1

R32	w	Bye, Bye			
R16	w	Garrone, Laura	6–0	6–1	
Q	w	Sukova, Helena	6–3	6–4	
S	w	Martinez, Conchita	6–3	6–3	
F	w	Navratilova, Martina	6–3	3–6	6–4

November

VIRGINIA SLIMS OF CALIFORNIA, *Oakland*

Indoor/Carpet   Draw: 32   Rank: S001   Seed: 1

R32	W	Bye, Bye			
R16	W	Javer, Monique	6–2	6–0	
Q	W	Harvey-Wild, Linda	6-0	6–2	
S	W	Maleeva-Fragnier,			
		Manuela	6–2	6–1	
F	L	Navratilova, Martina	6–3	3–6	6–3

November

VIRGINIA SLIMS OF PHILADELPHIA, *Philadelphia*

Indoor/Carpet   Draw: 32   Rank: S001   Seed: 1

R32	W	Bye, Bye			
R16	W	Werdel, Marianne	7–5	6–1	
Q	W	Garrison, Zina	7–6 (8–6)	6–0	
S	W	Sanchez Vicario,			
		Arantxa	6–1	6–2	
F	W	Capriati, Jennifer	7–5	6–1	

November

VIRGINIA SLIMS CHAMPIONSHIPS, *New York*

Indoor/Carpet   Draw: 16   Rank: S001   Seed: 1

R16	W	Halard, Julie	6–1	6–0
Q	W	Fernandez, Mary Joe	6–3	6–2

| S | W | Sabatini, Gabriela | 6–1 | 6–1 | | |
| F | W | Navratilova, Martina | 6–4 | 3–6 | 7–5 | 6–0 |

1992

January

AUSTRALIAN OPEN, *Melbourne*

Outdoor/Hard		Draw: 128		Rank: S001	Seed: 1
R128	W	Kijimuta, Akiko	6–2	6–0	
R64	W	Date, Kimiko	6–2	7–5	
R32	W	Basuki, Yayuk	6–1	6–1	
R16	W	Meskhi, Leila	6–4	4–6	6–2
Q	W	Huber, Anke	7–5	6–3	
S	W	Sanchez Vicario, Arantxa	6–2	6–2	
F	W	Fernandez, Mary Joe	6–2	6–3	

February

NOKIA GRAND PRIX, *Essen*

Indoor/Carpet		Draw: 32		Rank: S001	Seed: 1
R32	W	Bye, Bye			
R16	W	Kerek, Angela	6–2	6–2	
Q	W	Lindqvist, Catarina	6–3	6–2	
S	W	Pierce, Mary	6–0	6–1	
F	W	Fernandez, Mary Joe	6–0	6–3	

February–March

MATRIX ESSENTIALS EVERT CUP

Outdoor/Hard   Draw: 64   Rank: S001   Seed: 1

R64	W	Bye, Bye		
R32	W	Reinach, Elna	6–1	6–1
R16	W	Whitlinger, Tami	6–2	6–3
Q	W	Fernandez, Gigi	6–0	6–0
S	W	Maleeva, Katerina	6–1	6–0
F	W	Martinez, Conchita	6–3	6–1

March

LIPTON INTERNATIONAL PLAYERS' CHAMPIONSHIPS, *Key Biscayne*

Outdoor/Hard   Draw: 128   Rank: 0001   Seed: 1

R128	W	Bye, Bye		
R64	W	Benjamin, Camille	6–1	6–3
R32	W	Savchenko-Neilan, Larisa	6–0	6–4
R16	W	Zrubakova, Radka	6–1	6–2
Q	L	Capriati, Jennifer	6–2	7–6 (7–5)

April

VIRGINIA SLIMS OF HOUSTON, *Houston*

Outdoor/Clay   Draw: 32   Rank: 0001   Seed: 1

R32	W	Bye, Bye		
R16	W	Paz, Mercedes	6–0	6–0

Q	W	Fulco-Villella, Bettina 6–1	6–0	
S	W	Gildemeister, Laura 6–4	6–1	
F	W	Garrison, Zina 6–1	6–1	

April

OPEN SEAT OF SPAIN, *Barcelona*

Outdoor/Clay Draw: 32 Rank: 0001 Seed: 1

R32	W	Bye, Bye			
R16	W	Muns-Jagerman, Nicole	6–3	6–1	
Q	W	Pierce, Mary	7–6 (8–6)	6–4	
S	W	Maleeva-Fragnier, Manuela	6–3	6–1	
F	W	Sanchez Vicario, Arantxa	3–6	6–2	6–3

May

ITALIAN OPEN, *Rome*

Outdoor/Clay Draw: 64 Rank: 0001 Seed: 1

R64	W	Bye, Bye		
R32	W	Baudone, Natalia	6–0	6–4
R16	W	Cunningham, Carrie	6–0	6–1
Q	W	Meskhi, Leila	6–1	6–4
S	W	Coetzer, Amanda	6–0	6–4
F	L	Sabatini, Gabriela	7–5	6–4

June

FRENCH OPEN, *Paris*

Outdoor/Clay   Draw: 128   Rank: 0001   Seed: 1

R128	W	Mothes, Catherine	6–1	6–0	
R64	W	Kschwendt, Karin	6–2	6–2	
R32	W	Mcneil, Lori	6–0	6–1	
R16	W	Kijimuta, Akiko	6–1	3–6	6–4
Q	W	Capriati, Jennifer	6–2	6–2	
S	W	Sabatini, Gabriela	6–3	4–6	6–4
F	W	Graf, Steffi	6–2	3–6	10–8

July

WIMBLEDON, *London*

Outdoor/Grass   Draw: 128   Rank: 0001   Seed: 1

R128	W	Byrne, Jenny	6–2	6–2	
R64	W	Appelmans, Sabine	6–3	6–2	
R32	W	Gildemeister, Laura	6–4	6–1	
R16	W	Fernandez, Gigi	6–4	6–2	
Q	W	Tauziat, Nathalie	6–1	6–3	
S	W	Navratilova, Martina	6–2	6–7 (3–7)	6–4
F	L	Graf, Steffi	6–2	6–1	

August

VIRGINIA SLIMS OF LOS ANGELES, *Manhattan Beach*

Outdoor/Hard   Draw: 32   Rank: 0001   Seed: 1

R32	W	Bye, Bye			
R16	W	Habsudova, Karina	6–2	6–2	
Q	W	Frazier, Amy	6–2	6–0	
S	W	Sanchez Vicario, Arantxa	6–3	6–2	
F	L	Navratilova, Martina	6–4	6–2	

August

CANADIAN OPEN, *Montreal*

Outdoor/Hard   Draw: 64   Rank: 0001   Seed: 1

R64	W	Bye, Bye			
R32	W	Werdel, Marianne	6–2	6–4	
R16	W	Sawamatsu, Naoko	6–1	6–2	
Q	W	Hy, Patricia	6–1	4–6	6–1
S	W	McNeil, Lori	6–3	6–4	
F	L	Sanchez Vicario, Arantxa	6–3	4–6	6–4

September

US OPEN, *New York*

Outdoor/Hard   Draw: 128   Rank: 0001   Seed: 1

R128	W	Keller, Audra	6–1	6–0
R64	W	Raymond, Lisa	7–5	6–0

R32	W	Porwik, Claudia	6–4	6–0
R16	W	Fernandez, Gigi	6–1	6–2
Q	W	Hy, Patricia	6–1	6–2
S	W	Fernandez, Mary Joe	6–3	6–2
F	W	Sanchez Vicario, Arantxa	6–3	6–3

September

NICHIREI INTERNATIONAL, *Tokyo*

Indoor/Carpet   Draw: 32   Rank: 0001   Seed: 1

R32	W	Bye, Bye			
R16	W	Wang, Shi-Ting	6–0	6–1	
Q	W	Sawamatsu, Naoko	6–1	6–0	
S	W	Fernandez, Mary Joe	6–0	3–6	6–4
F	W	Sabatini, Gabriela	6–2	6–0	

November

BANK OF WEST CLASSIC, *Oakland*

Indoor/Carpet   Draw: 32   Rank: 0001   Seed: 1

R32	W	Bye, Bye		
R16	W	Rehe, Stephanie	6–4	6–1
Q	W	Majoli, Iva	6–3	6–1
S	W	Huber, Anke	6–2	6–3
F	W	Navratilova, Martina	6–3	6–4

November

VIRGINIA SLIMS CHAMPIONSHIPS, *New York*

Indoor/Carpet   Draw: 16   Rank: 0001   Seed: 1

R16	W	Tauziat, Nathalie	6–1	6–2	
Q	W	Novotna, Jana	3–6	6–4	6–1
S	W	Sabatini, Gabriela	7–6	6–1	
F	W	Navratilova, Martina	7–5	6–3	6–1

1993

January

AUSTRALIAN OPEN, *Melbourne*

Outdoor/Hard   Draw: 128   Rank: 0001   Seed: 1

R128	W	Pizzichini, Gloria	6–1	6–1	
R64	W	Strandlund, Maria	6–2	6–0	
R32	W	Fendick, Patty	6–1	6–0	
R16	W	Tauziat, Nathalie	6–2	6–0	
Q	W	Halard, Julie	6–2	6–7 (5–7)	6–0
S	W	Sabatini, Gabriela	6–1	6–2	
F	W	Graf, Steffi	4–6	6–3	6–2

February

VIRGINIA SLIMS OF CHICAGO, *Chicago*

Indoor/Carpet   Draw: 32   Rank: 0001   Seed: 1

R32	W	Bye, Bye			
R16	W	Po, Kimberly	6–1	6–2	
Q	W	Schultz, Brenda	4–6	7–6 (7–4)	6–4
S	W	Fernandez, Mary Joe	6–3	6–0	
F	W	Navratilova, Martina	3–6	6–2	6–1

February

FRENCH OPEN, *Paris*

Indoor/Carpet   Draw: 32   Rank: 0001   Seed: 1

R32	W	Porwik, Claudia	6–1	6–2	
R16	W	Wiesner, Judith	6–1	6–4	
Q	W	Pierce, Mary	6–2	6–2	
S	W	Martinez, Conchita	6–1	6–1	
F	L	Navratilova, Martina	6–3	4–6	7–6 (7–3)

May

CITIZEN CUP, *Hamburg*

Outdoor/Clay   Draw: 32   Rank: 0001   Seed: 1

R32	W	Strandlund, Maria	6–2	6–2	
R16	W	Tarabini, Patricia	6–2	6–2	
Q	L	Maleeva, Magdalena	4–6	3–4	Ret

1995

August

CANADIAN OPEN, *Toronto*

Outdoor/Hard   Draw: 64   Rank: 0001   Seed: 1

R64	W	Bye, Bye			
R32	W	Po, Kimberly	6–0	6–3	
R16	W	Tauziat, Nathalie	6–2	6–2	
Q	W	Huber, Anke	6–3	6–2	
S	W	Sabatini, Gabriela	6–1	6–0	
F	W	Coetzer, Amanda	6–0	6–1	

September

US OPEN, *New York*

Outdoor/Hard   Draw: 128   Rank: 0001   Seed: 2

R128	W	Dragomir, Ruxandra	6–3	6–1	
R64	W	De Lone, Erika	6–2	6–1	
R32	W	Kamio, Yone	6–1	6–1	
R16	W	Huber, Anke	6–1	6–4	
Q	W	Novotna, Jana	7–6 (7–5)	6–2	
S	W	Martinez, Conchita	6–2	6–2	
F	L	Graf, Steffi	7–6 (8–6)	0–6	6–3

1996

January

PETERS NSW OPEN, *Sydney*

Outdoor/Hard   Draw: 32   Rank: 0001   Seed: 1

R32	w	Bye, Bye			
R16	w	Van Roost,			
		Dominique	6–1	6–2	
Q	w	De Swardt, Mariaan	6–3	6–2	
S	w	Schultz-McCarthy,			
		Brenda	7–6 (8–6)	6–4	
F	w	Davenport, Lindsay	4–6	7–6 (9–7)	6–3

January

AUSTRALIAN OPEN, *Melbourne*

Outdoor/Hard   Draw: 128   Rank: 0001   Seed: 1

R128	w	Lee, Janet	6–3	6–0	
R64	w	Studenikova,			
		Katarina	6–1	6–1	
R32	w	Halard-Decugis, Julie	7–5	6–0	
R16	w	Sawamatsu, Naoko	6–1	6–3	
Q	w	Majoli, Iva	6–1	6–2	
S	w	Rubin, Chanda	6–7 (2–7)	6–1	7–5
F	w	Huber, Anke	6–4	6–1	

February

PAN PACIFIC, *Tokyo*

Indoor/Carpet   Draw: 32   Rank: 0001   Seed: 1

R32	W	Bye, Bye			
R16	W	Spirlea, Irina	6–4	6–2	
Q	L	Majoli, Iva	1–6	7–6	6–4

Scores in brackets denote tie-breakers.

INDEX